THE OPIOID EPIDEMIC

Hal Marcovitz

ReferencePoint
Press®

San Diego, CA

About the Author
Hal Marcovitz is a former newspaper reporter and columnist who lives in Chalfont, Pennsylvania. He is the author of nearly two hundred books for young readers.

For more information, contact:
ReferencePoint Press, Inc.
PO Box 27779
San Diego, CA 92198
www.ReferencePointPress.com

LIBRARY OF CONGRESS CATALOGING-IN-PUBLICATION DATA

Name: Marcovitz, Hal, author.
Title: The Opioid Epidemic/by Hal Marcovitz.
Description: San Diego, CA: ReferencePoint Press, Inc., 2018. | Includes
  bibliographical references and index.
Identifiers: LCCN 2017017982 (print) | LCCN 2017024660 (ebook) | ISBN
  9781682823002 (eBook) | ISBN 9781682822999 (hardback)
Subjects: LCSH: Opioid abuse--Juvenile literature. | Drug abuse--Juvenile
  literature.
Classification: LCC RC568.O45 (ebook) | LCC RC568.O45 M37 2018 (print) | DDC
  362.29/3--dc23
LC record available at https://lccn.loc.gov/2017017982

CONTENTS

The Victims of Opioids

The pop star known as Prince burst onto the music scene in the late 1970s. Over the course of the next four decades, Prince established himself as a truly incandescent performer. He scored many hits and toured widely over the course of his career, engaging his fans with electrifying performances featuring hot beats, colorful costumes, and scintillating dance moves.

By 2016 the wear and tear of touring had taken its toll on Prince's body. At the age of fifty-seven, he still maintained a heavy touring schedule even though he suffered from debilitating knee and hip pain. To help him endure the performances, Prince relied on the prescription opioid painkiller fentanyl. The drug deadens feelings of pain by providing a narcotic-like sensation.

On April 21, 2016, Prince was found dead in his mansion near Minneapolis, Minnesota. A few days later authorities released the cause of death: He had suffered a fatal overdose of fentanyl. The drug had slowed down his respiratory system, depriving his body of oxygen. As authorities pursued an investigation into the cause of death, they learned the pop star had been addicted to opioid painkillers, taking them several times a day—and not just to counter pain spikes following a concert.

Says Zachary Siegel, a columnist for the website Daily Beast and a former opioid addict himself,

> Part of the reason fentanyl is so dangerous is that the lethal dose is so close to the therapeutic dose, making any margin of error deadly. In an effort to kill the pain, maybe [Prince] began taking too much. What's also possible is

that Prince loved the feeling produced by a head high on [opioids]. Fentanyl, after all, is the Ferrari of painkillers. Its onset is rapid, and before you know it you're somewhere in the clouds, so numb and weak you can't even make a fist.[1]

More People Taking Opioids

Although Prince's death garnered international headlines, the story of his addiction to opioids is not unique. A 2016 poll conducted by the Kaiser Family Foundation, which explores issues relevant to people's health, reported that 44 percent of Americans know somebody who is addicted to prescription opioid painkillers. Moreover, even though the dangers of opioid abuse have emerged in the public consciousness, more and more people are obtaining prescriptions for opioids to deal with their pain. A 2017 poll by National Public Radio (NPR) reported that 57 percent of Americans have received prescriptions for opioid painkillers at least once in their lives—a 3 percent increase since 2014 when NPR last commissioned a poll on the issue. "The drugs are like a two-edged sword," says Ron Ozminkowski, vice president of IBM Watson Health, which analyzes health trends. "They're great for people who really need them for heavy duty pain, but they come with addiction risk and side effects."[2]

> "The drugs are like a two-edged sword. They're great for people who really need them for heavy duty pain, but they come with addiction risk and side effects."[2]
>
> —Ron Ozminkowski, health care analyst

Painkillers such as fentanyl, hydrocodone, and oxycodone have a lot in common with the street drug heroin. All are opioids. All provide users with narcotic effects. All are highly addictive. And all can very easily lead to death through overdose. Says Andrew Kolodny, chief medical officer at the New York City–based addiction counseling center Phoenix House, "Anyone can get hooked, even those using the drug legitimately to combat pain."[3]

Anyone Can Be a Victim

As the statistics show, opioids have become so prevalent in society, virtually anyone can become addicted—ranging from internationally

In 2016 pop superstar Prince was found dead in his home from a fatal overdose of the prescription painkiller fentanyl. He had been using painkillers for years to combat debilitating knee and hip pain and had developed an addiction.

known pop stars such as Prince to young people who may live in American cities, suburbs, or small towns. "The drugs don't differentiate based on your station in life or why you're using them," says Kolodny. "The effect on the brain is the same."[4]

Andrew Cuomo, who grew up in Camden, New Jersey (and who is of no relation to the New York governor of the same name), started taking fentanyl as well as other prescription painkillers at the age of nineteen to recover from a back injury he sustained in an automobile accident. As Cuomo recovered from his injuries, he discovered that many of his friends were also taking fentanyl as well as heroin. Soon, Cuomo moved on to heroin himself, becoming addicted to the drug. And he continued taking heroin even though some of his friends had died from heroin overdoses. "I lost eight friends in less than a year, and I mean close friends, not just people that I knew,"[5] says Cuomo.

Cuomo entered drug rehabilitation in 2009 and was able to kick his habit to opioids. Other people he knew were not so fortunate. "Most of the people I grew up with who were my friends, 80 percent are dead," says Cuomo. "One thing that always kept me going was I wasn't going to give up."[6]

The cases of Prince and Cuomo illustrate how opioid abuse can affect virtually anyone—from a wealthy celebrity to a teenager growing up in a New Jersey city. Both started taking opioid painkillers to deal with pain, but both also fell victim to the narcotic and addictive qualities of the drugs—a circumstance that has contributed to the growing opioid epidemic in America and elsewhere.

> "I lost eight friends in less than a year, and I mean close friends, not just people that I knew."[5]
>
> —Andrew Cuomo, former opioid addict

CHAPTER ONE

A Problem of Epidemic Proportions

Over the past quarter-century, the abuse of drugs known as opioids—prescription painkillers as well as the illegal drug heroin—has emerged as a significant public health issue. According to the American Society of Addiction Medicine, in 2015 more than 2 million Americans were addicted to prescription opioid painkillers while another half-million were addicted to heroin. Moreover, according to the US Centers for Disease Control and Prevention (CDC), in 2014 more than twenty-eight thousand Americans died of opioid overdoses.

Other countries report similar statistics. In Canada, about one hundred thousand people a year are believed to abuse opioids, according to a 2015 study by the Canadian Centre on Substance Abuse. And in Europe, a 2010 assessment of drug abuse in thirty nations compiled by the European Monitoring Centre for Drugs and Drug Addiction found that more than 1.3 million people abuse opioids.

In 2016 a report by the US Department of Health and Human Services (HHS) stated:

> Our nation is in the midst of an unprecedented opioid epidemic. More people died from drug overdoses in 2014 than in any year on record, and the majority of drug overdose deaths (more than six out of ten) involved an opioid. Since 1999, the rate of overdose deaths involving opioids—including prescription opioid pain relievers and heroin—nearly quadrupled, and over 165,000 people have died from prescription opioid overdoses. Prescription pain medication deaths remain far too high.[7]

What Are Opioids?

Despite the devastating consequences of opioid abuse, prescription opioid painkillers are nevertheless very effective for what they are designed to do: deaden severe pain in patients who have suffered injuries or are afflicted with diseases such as cancer. However, due to the narcotic qualities of the drugs, many patients find themselves addicted to the substances—abusing them, often to the point of suffering fatal overdoses. Heroin, on the other hand, has long been an illegal drug and for decades has been responsible for rampant addiction, tortured lives, and overdose deaths.

Opioid painkillers include such drugs as methadone, hydrocodone, fentanyl, codeine, and oxycodone—but most are better known by the brands under which they are marketed by the pharmaceutical companies that make them. Among the better-known brands are Vicodin, Percocet, OxyContin, and Dilaudid. Tylenol 3, a prescription-only form of the familiar over-the-counter painkiller Tylenol, contains codeine. These drugs are synthetic opioids, meaning they have been formulated with combinations of chemicals.

Unlike these well-known synthetic opioids, heroin is a natural drug. It is distilled from the liquid found within the seeds of the opium plant.

The Opium Trade

The opioid epidemic that afflicts modern society can trace its roots to 1680, when the British pharmacist Thomas Sydenham developed the first medical use of the opium plant. He combined it with sherry wine and some local herbs to make the drug laudanum, which was used as a painkiller. And in 1805 German pharmacist Friedrich Sertuerner distilled an even more powerful painkiller from the opium plant. Known as morphine, the drug is typically injected into patients. Sertuerner named the drug after Morpheus, the ancient Greek god of dreams.

Morphine helped revolutionize the practice of battlefield medicine, giving doctors a quick and effective method of reducing the pain suffered by wounded soldiers. But morphine is also a highly addictive drug. Following the American Civil War, tens of thousands of soldiers returned to their homes—their battlefield wounds healed but, nevertheless, addicted to morphine.

Most Drug Overdose Deaths Are Linked to Opioids

Opioids are now the primary cause of drug overdose deaths in the United States. Drug overdose deaths linked to opioids (both prescription and illicit) have quadrupled since 1999, according to the Centers for Disease Control and Prevention (CDC). In 2015 alone, the CDC notes, opioids were involved in 33,091 deaths. That same year, the states with the highest rates of drug overdose deaths were West Virginia, New Hampshire, Kentucky, Ohio, and Rhode Island. Several other states, particularly in the Northeast and South, experienced large increases in drug overdose death rates between 2014 and 2015.

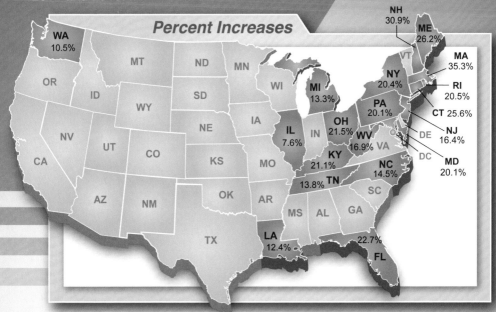

Source: Centers for Disease Control and Prevention, "Drug Overdose Death Data," December 16, 2016. www.cdc.gov.

By the late 1800s, the practice of smoking opium was well embedded in world culture. American cowboy icons Kit Carson and Wild Bill Hickok were opium smokers. In 1890 the US Congress took its first step to regulate opium use—not by banning the drug, but by imposing a tax on the opium trade. In 1895 the drug known as heroin first surfaced in society—not as an illegal drug but as a painkiller. With twice the potency of morphine, it was formulated from the opium plant by the German pharmaceutical company Bayer, which is today known mostly as a manufacturer of aspirin. Heinrich Dreser, the chemist who formulated the drug, called it diacetylmorphine, but Bayer sold the drug under a brand name: Heroin.

The addictive qualities of the drugs soon became evident to lawmakers. Starting in 1909, Congress adopted a number of laws designed to regulate opium and heroin in order to cut down on use of the drugs. In 1923 the Narcotics Division of the US Treasury Department—the first government agency specifically tasked with combating the illegal drug trade—banned all legal sales of narcotics, including heroin. But just because the government said heroin was now illegal did not mean heroin addicts no longer needed the drug. Instead, the ban on legal sales of heroin drove the trade underground.

Junkies on American Streets

By the 1940s, heroin trafficking had been largely taken over by international criminal gangs. The French city of Marseilles became a major center for illegal labs. Asian opium was shipped to Marseilles where it was processed into heroin, smuggled across the Atlantic Ocean, and sold on American streets to drug users.

During the 1950s and 1960s, the image of the heroin addict emerged in American culture: A rail-thin drug abuser living on the streets of big cities such as New York, Chicago, or Los Angeles. Known as junkies—a common street name for heroin is junk—heroin addicts often survive by panhandling or committing petty crimes, using whatever money they can raise to buy their drugs from street dealers known as pushers. The drug is usually administered by needle: junkies jab themselves in the arms, or between the toes, or anywhere else they can find veins that haven't collapsed due to years of abuse. In 1972 the noted science writer Edward M. Brecher described the typical heroin addict:

> To be a confirmed drug addict is to be one of the walking dead. . . . The teeth have rotted out, the appetite is lost, and the stomach and intestines don't function properly. . . . Boils and abscesses plague the skin; gnawing pain racks the body. Nerves snap; vicious twitching develops. Imaginary

and fantastic fears blight the mind and sometimes complete insanity results. Often times, too, death comes . . . Such is the torment of being a drug addict; such is the plague of being one of the walking dead.[8]

Birth of Synthetic Opioids

Heroin was a highly addictive and abused drug—but it could also relieve pain. Physicians and pharmaceutical companies wondered whether legal and nonaddictive drugs could be produced that could mimic heroin's ability to reduce pain. Instead of using the opium plant, which had been banned by Congress decades earlier, these companies looked to employ chemicals to formulate their drugs by synthetic methods. The first synthetic opioid painkiller approved for sale in America was codeine. Actually, codeine dates back to 1832 when a French chemist, Pierre Robiquet, synthesized the drug from opium seeds. The drug's name can be traced to the Greek word *kodeia*, which means "poppy head." However, after opium was outlawed in America and elsewhere, pharmaceutical companies looked for ways to make the drug without the use of opium. In the 1970s they discovered a way to synthesize the drug from coal tar, which is a byproduct of coal processing and a common ingredient in medicinal skin treatments.

But codeine is a relatively mild opioid, and the search continued for drugs that could provide even deeper relief. Meanwhile, researchers raised the question of whether drugs that could mimic heroin's pain-relieving qualities would also turn out to be addictive. At first, doctors who advocated for the development of more effective synthetic opioids predicted little probability that patients could become addicted to them. Wrote pain management specialists Russell Portenoy and Kathleen Foley in a 1986 issue of the medical journal *Pain*, "We conclude that

"We conclude that opioid maintenance therapy can be a safe . . . and more humane alternative to the options of surgery or no treatment in those patients with intractable non-malignant pain."[9]

—Russell Portenoy and Kathleen Foley, pain management specialists

Union Army soldiers during the Civil War recover from surgical amputations. They were given morphine, a powerful opioid, for their pain. Many of them eventually became addicted to morphine.

opioid maintenance therapy can be a safe . . . and more humane alternative to the options of surgery or no treatment in those patients with intractable non-malignant pain and no history of drug abuse."[9]

In 1984 the German pharmaceutical company Knoll Pharmaceuticals produced Vicodin, an intensely effective pain reliever. In the years since Vicodin was introduced to the market, the business of making and selling opioid painkillers has emerged as a huge industry. Anybody who has been tackled hard on the football field, breaking an arm; or has had a tooth extracted; or suffers from the chronic pain of arthritis wants only one thing: to end the pain. Pharmaceutical companies recognized the potential market for drugs that could effectively eliminate pain, envisioning profits in the billions of dollars. And so by developing Vicodin and the other synthetic opioids, pharmaceutical companies found a way to respond to the demands by patients and their doctors to address the painful effects of severe injuries and diseases while also ensuring themselves enormous profits.

One of the drawbacks of Vicodin and other prescription opioids is the duration of their effects: Typically, the drugs wear off after three or four hours, meaning the patients need multiple doses a day to relieve their pain. In 1995, the American pharmaceutical company Purdue Pharma developed OxyContin, a form of the opioid oxycodone. Purdue found a way to develop a time-release mechanism in the drug's chemistry, meaning the pain-killing effect of the drug could be stretched over a period as long as twelve hours. "They don't wear out; they go on working; they do not have serious medical side effects," a doctor explained in a Purdue promotional video. "So, these drugs, which I repeat, are our best, strongest pain medications, should be used much more than they are for patients in pain."[10]

> "So, these drugs, which I repeat, are our best, strongest pain medications, should be used much more than they are for patients in pain."[10]
>
> —Purdue Pharma promotional video

OxyContin's time-release feature proved to be particularly popular among doctors who did not want to see their patients swallowing a half-dozen or more opioid pills per day. And sales numbers for OxyContin reflect the drug's popularity. In 1995, the first year OxyContin went on the market, the drug earned $45 million for Purdue. By 2000, OxyContin sales surpassed the $1 billion mark. And in 2010, OxyContin earned $3 billion for its manufacturer.

More Pills than People

While sales of OxyContin have increased dramatically since its introduction, in fact, virtually all synthetic opioid drugs are used widely. A 2016 report issued by the San Francisco, California–based health care consulting company Castlight Health found that in 2012 doctors wrote 259 million prescriptions for opioid painkillers—nearly enough prescriptions to provide every American with his or her own bottle of pills. Moreover, a CDC report found that in some states, there are more opioid prescriptions than there are people. In 2012 in Alabama and Tennessee, for example, the CDC reported that there were about 143 opioid prescriptions written for every

Women and Opioids

American women make up one of the fastest growing groups of people who are becoming addicted to opioid painkillers. According to the US Centers for Disease Control and Prevention (CDC), the annual death rate for women who have overdosed on opioid painkillers has increased by 400 percent since 1999 (versus a 265 percent increase for men). About eighteen women die every day by overdosing on opioid painkillers, according to the CDC. "Deaths from prescription painkiller overdose among women have risen more sharply than among men," stated a 2013 CDC report. "This rise relates closely to increased prescribing of these drugs during the past decade."

As the CDC reported, women are using opioids for conditions that traditionally did not require such treatment. For instance, a 2017 study by the University of Pittsburgh found opioids are now prescribed for women recovering from the ordeal of childbirth. According to the report, about 18,000 women among 165,000 who were studied went home from the hospital with opioid prescriptions after delivering their babies. In years past, new mothers may have been advised by their doctors to take over-the-counter painkillers, such as Advil or Tylenol, or treat their post-childbirth pain with nondrug therapies, such as heat or sitz baths.

The study suggested that the increased use of opioids for childbirth-related pain has led many women into addiction. The study found 2,600 cases in which women renewed their opioid prescriptions two months after childbirth, even though most of those women had no pain-causing conditions in their medical records.

US Centers for Disease Control and Prevention, "Prescription Painkiller Overdoses: A Growing Epidemic, Especially Among Women," *CDC Vital Signs*, July 2013. www.cdc.gov.

---

100 people. (According to the report, Hawaii had the least number of prescriptions: about 52 prescriptions for every 100 people—or, roughly, one prescription for every other person in the state.) In total, HHS reported, some 650,000 prescriptions for opioid painkillers are filled in America every day.

Statistics suggest that all sorts of people are prescribed opioid painkillers. A recent study published in the *Journal of the American Medical Association* found that doctors have prescribed opioid painkillers to patients ranging in age from young children to senior citizens. According to the study, 0.7 percent of opioid prescriptions were written for patients below the age of 9; 11.7 percent for patients between the ages of 10 and 29; 13.6

percent for patients between the ages of 30 and 39; 45.7 percent for patients between the ages of 40 and 59; and 28.3 percent were written for patients 60 and older. When those statistics are compared with the numbers reported by Castlight Health, it can be stated that a total of 0.7 percent of the 259 million opioid painkiller prescriptions that are written each year—or about 18 million prescriptions—are issued to children age 9 or younger.

In fact, young people have for years recognized the narcotic powers of opioid painkillers. In 2002, Monitoring the Future, a

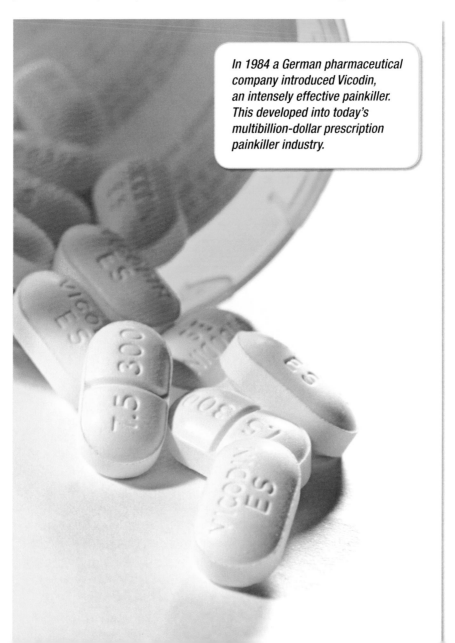

In 1984 a German pharmaceutical company introduced Vicodin, an intensely effective painkiller. This developed into today's multibillion-dollar prescription painkiller industry.

University of Michigan program that studies the habits of young people, began tracking how teenagers in the eighth, tenth, and twelfth grades abuse opioid painkillers. In that first year, Monitoring the Future found that 2.5 percent of eighth-grade students, 6.9 percent of tenth-grade students, and 9.6 percent of twelfth-grade students had experimented with Vicodin at least once in the prior year. Monitoring the Future also looked at OxyContin use that year, finding that 1.3 percent of eighth-grade students, 3 percent of tenth-grade students, and 4 percent of twelfth-grade students had used OxyContin at least once in the previous year.

In 2016 the Monitoring the Future statistics indicated that Vicodin use among young people had fallen, but OxyContin use had dropped just slightly. The study found that in the previous year, 0.8 percent of eighth-grade students, 1.7 percent of tenth-grade students, and 2.9 percent of twelfth-grade students had used Vicodin. As for OxyContin, the statistics showed 0.9 percent of eighth-grade students, 2.1 percent of tenth-grade students, and 3.4 percent of twelfth-grade students had used the drug in the previous year.

Road to Addiction

As those statistics show, the consumption of opioid painkillers—both legally and illegally—has emerged as a routine part of living for many Americans as well as people in other countries. And despite the prediction of some pain experts in the 1980s that opioid painkillers would not be widely abused, opioid addiction is now regarded as a serious public health threat. Opioid abusers can be found in virtually all corners of American society—in the cities and suburbs as well as in small towns and rural communities. And as many people are learning, the consequences of opioid addiction can be quite severe.

In 2016 Judy Jenkins dropped by her daughter's home in northern Virginia for a visit. Jenkins's daughter, Lydia Huebner, had long been unable to maintain a happy life. Since childhood, Huebner struggled with obesity. She was also a heavy drinker as well as a dedicated user of marijuana and cocaine. Huebner also had difficulty holding on to jobs. At some point, Jenkins knew, her daughter had transitioned from alcohol, marijuana, and cocaine to abusing opioid painkillers. Huebner also complained of chronic pain and often obtained prescriptions for opioid painkillers from doctors, but her mother suspected Huebner was faking her pain and using the pills not for their pain-killing qualities but to achieve narcotic highs. "She could convince anyone to give her drugs,"[11] Jenkins says.

Jenkins knocked on the door to her daughter's town house several times before realizing that something must be terribly wrong inside. She found the landlord and convinced him to open the door. Rushing into her daughter's home, she found Huebner on the floor, several empty pill bottles strewn around her body. Jenkins, a retired nurse, performed cardiopulmonary resuscitation in an effort to revive her daughter, but it was too late—Huebner had already died. The cause of death was later attributed to an overdose of opioids. "As a nurse, you don't want anyone to die," Jenkins says. "As a mother, you don't want to watch any of your children die because it's the wrong order of things."[12]

The Menace of Heroin

Just as abuse of opioid painkillers can often lead to fatal consequences, heroin remains a dangerous drug that is widely used—and not just by junkies on the streets of big cities. In St. Charles County, Missouri, a suburb of St. Louis, Gee Vigna walked into her seventeen-year-old daughter Nicky's room one morning to wake her for school. She found the girl unresponsive.

> "She was completely gray, her eyes were rolled back in the back of her head and she was frothing at the mouth."[13]
>
> —Gee Vigna, mother of teenage heroin user

"She was completely gray, her eyes were rolled back in the back of her head and she was frothing at the mouth," Vigna said. "I screamed for my husband . . . and we're shaking her and we're shaking her. I'm running around the house trying to find a phone and he says to me, 'She's dead already.'" The Vignas called an ambulance. Fortunately, Nicky had not died—the emergency medical technicians were able to revive her. "The EMT asked me, 'What kind of drugs does your daughter take?' And I said, 'She doesn't take drugs,' and he said, 'She has track marks all over her arms . . . your daughter is a heroin addict.' I just looked at him. As a parent I just felt like a total idiot and I said, 'There's just no way.'"[13]

Higher Addiction Rates in Rural Areas

Although people who abuse opioids can live anywhere, recent studies have shown that addiction rates are highest in rural areas. A 2016 report issued by the San Francisco, California–based health care consulting company Castlight Health identified the twenty-five American communities where opioid abuse is highest. Such big cities as New York, Chicago, and Los Angeles did not appear on the list. Rather, small towns—such as Elmira, New York; Fayetteville, North Carolina; and Killeen, Texas—made the list of top opioid abuse communities. In Elmira, which led the list, the Castlight study found that 55 percent of patients who have received prescriptions for opioid painkillers have abused the drugs.

Moreover, a 2016 study by the Maine Rural Health Research Center found that rural residents tend to abuse opioids at higher rates than urban residents because they tend to suffer more workplace injuries. Also, the study said, rural Americans typically have less access to physicians and, therefore, their opioid use is likely to receive less monitoring from doctors. Says addictions specialist Kathleen Brady, professor of psychiatry at the Medical University of South Carolina, "Here in South Carolina . . . more people work in manual labor jobs that can lead to injury and pain and the use of [opioid] prescription drugs. The problem is made worse because there are fewer physicians and fewer treatment options in rural areas."

Quoted in Aaron Levin, "Overcoming Opioid Abuse in Rural U.S. Requires Varied Approach," *Psychiatric News*, March 24, 2016. http://psychnews.psychiatryonline.org.

As the cases of Lydia Huebner and Nicky Vigna illustrate, opioids are a danger to all who abuse them. Certainly, that fact was evident to the American lawmakers in the early years of the twentieth century when they adopted the first measures to regulate and eventually outlaw opium and heroin.

But pain has never gone away. People who have been injured in accidents or on the athletic field or by slipping on the ice often find themselves in intense pain. So do people who suffer from illnesses such as cancer. These patients want nothing more than for the pain to end. Sadly, the injuries or illnesses that have led them to use Vicodin, Percocet, and OxyContin often lead them down the road to addiction.

CHAPTER TWO

How Do People Get Addicted?

Opioid painkillers are usually ingested in pill form. In the case of heroin, the drug is typically liquefied from a powder and injected into the body with a needle—although users are also known to inhale the powder through their noses or smoke it in pipes or rolled in cigarette papers. Regardless of how the user ingests opioids, they are soaked up by the blood, which carries the drugs on a quick journey through the body.

Although opioid painkillers are very effective in relieving pain, the drugs have nothing to do with healing the injury or curing the illness that causes the pain. A patient who swallows an opioid pill after breaking an ankle would not find the drug heading for the source of the injury where it enhances healing or deadens the pain just in the ankle. Rather, opioids are carried to the brain, which, essentially, makes the body believe it hasn't been injured.

As soon as the drugs arrive in the brain, they attach themselves to clusters of molecules known as opioid receptors. The arrival of the opioid drug then sparks the brain into releasing dopamine, a chemical that is known as a neurotransmitter. Dopamine helps people think, move their limbs, and feel emotions—particularly pleasure. Anybody who has heard a favorite song on the radio, enjoyed a tasty meal, laughed at a joke, or opened a birthday gift has experienced something of a "dopamine rush."

In the case of opioids, the dopamine rush is so intense that feelings of deep and throbbing pain are made to disappear. And so are virtually all other feelings, thoughts, and emotions that people may find troubling. "My brain on [opioids] felt like pure heaven," says Joani Gammill, who started using opioids as a nursing student in college. "Euphoria and a sense of well-being enveloped my experience, and I felt truly happy for the first time in my life."[14]

Developing Drug Dependencies

All opioids spark the release of dopamine, but not all opioids help release dopamine at the same pace. A heroin user may feel the rush of dopamine within seconds of injecting the needle into his or her arm. Somebody who consumes Percocet may have to wait fifteen minutes for the dopamine rush. Vicodin typically takes about thirty minutes before users start feeling the effects. The time it takes for the drugs to take hold, as well as the length of the drugs' effects, depends on how the medications are formulated by their manufacturers.

Moreover, the effectiveness and length of the drugs' pain-killing qualities have a lot to do with the size of their dosages. Doctors would ordinarily prescribe a much stronger dose of an opioid painkiller for the most severe conditions, such as cancer, than they would to reduce the pain emanating from a sprained ankle. And most people do follow their doctors' orders: They take their opioid painkillers for only as long as they need them. As their injuries heal and their pain recedes, they take fewer pills or smaller doses and, when they feel better, they stop taking them.

However, some people find it very difficult to give up the intense feelings of pleasure brought on by a dopamine rush—and it is these users who frequently become addicted. "It can cause the person to want to recreate this sensation over and over again, and eventually, they start to need to stimulate it in order to avoid becoming sick by not taking," says Massachusetts physician Peter Grinspoon, who has firsthand knowledge of opioid effects, having spent nine years addicted to Percocet. "On an [opioid], things can feel dream-like and unbelievably euphoric. You don't feel physical or mental pain as much."[15]

Opioid addiction occurs because people develop dependencies on their drugs—they find they can't function normally without

> "On an [opioid], things can feel dream-like and unbelievably euphoric. You don't feel physical or mental pain as much."[15]
>
> —Peter Grinspoon, Massachusetts physician and former opioid addict

Some opioids are ingested in pill form. However, heroin is a powder that can be liquefied and injected in the body with a needle, or can be smoked.

consuming the opioid. People who take too many opioids over too long a period often find the chemistry in their brains changing: Since the dopamine produced by their brains is sparked by opioid drugs, eventually their brains stop producing dopamine on their own. Only with a kick-start from the opioid will the body produce the neurotransmitter. "If you repeatedly ingest drugs like [opioids], your brain will adapt," says Gammill. "It has come to depend on the large influx of dopamine from the drugs and so stops producing dopamine naturally. This adaptation has the effects of not only reducing or eliminating the feelings of pleasure we would experience through normal activities but also of creating a powerful motivation to use the drug—if only to feel normal. At this point, addiction has now taken hold."[16]

The Heroin High

As an opioid, heroin also provides a dopamine rush and—as with painkillers—a dependency on the drug can be developed very quickly. Many people who find themselves addicted to heroin typically did not start taking the drug to kill the pain of a broken rib or extracted tooth. Heroin has not been a legal drug in America for nearly a century. Therefore, for many years people who used heroin experimented with the drug solely for the euphoric effect—the high—and for no other reason.

However, recent studies have indicated that many people move on to heroin after first taking opioid painkillers. A 2014 study published in the *Journal of the American Medical Association (JAMA)* found increasing evidence to suggest that many

Doctors Often Overprescribe Opioids

Since evidence of the opioid epidemic first surfaced, the medical community has shouldered a great deal of the blame. Experts say doctors have been overprescribing the drugs—in other words, writing too many prescriptions for their patients. In fact, a 2016 study by the National Safety Council, a nonprofit group that promotes policies that enhance health and safety, concluded that a staggering 99 percent of doctors write prescriptions for opioid painkillers for periods of time beyond what their patients need—usually just seven days. The study found physicians almost always write prescriptions for opioid painkillers in doses that are stronger than what their patients need to address their pain. Also, the study reported that opioid prescriptions are typically written for many ailments that can be effectively addressed with non-opioid painkillers, such as over-the-counter products like Tylenol, Motrin, or Advil.

Among those ailments, the study said, is pain caused by toothaches. "Studies have shown that once we get beyond seven days of these [opioid] prescriptions for acute pain, the outcomes become much worse," says Donald Teater, medical adviser for the National Safety Council. "[Patients] get on these for a long time and have a hard time getting off them."

Quoted in John Keilman, "Almost All Doctors Routinely Overprescribe Pain Pills: Survey," *Chicago Tribune*, March 24, 2016. www.chicagotribune.com.

people transition to heroin from opioid painkillers—either because their doctors cut off their opioid prescriptions or because heroin is cheaper. (On the black market, drug dealers may sell a single opioid pill for thirty dollars, whereas a dose of heroin may cost fifteen dollars.) Says the *JAMA* study, "Reports from law enforcement and substance abuse treatment professionals have long suggested that many individuals who become addicted to prescription painkillers eventually move on to heroin when it becomes too difficult or expensive to access prescription opioids."[17]

> "It will cling to you like an obsessed lover. The rush of the hit and the way you'll want more, as if you were being deprived of air—that's how it will trap you."[19]
>
> —Sam, a fifteen-year-old heroin addict

For the first-time heroin user, a feeling of nausea might accompany the dopamine rush, but that ailment passes quickly as the drug takes effect. The rush provided by heroin arrives within seconds if injected (or about fifteen minutes if sniffed or smoked), providing the user with an intense feeling of euphoria. After a minute or so, the initial rush wears off but the high continues. According to the addiction treatment website TheGoodDrugsGuide.com,

Once the initial rush has passed, there can be a feeling of heaviness, as though your bones have melted down into your feet; followed by a feeling of distance from events around you, as though you've been wrapped in cotton wool. Heroin sedates the central nervous system clouding mental function and making you feel drowsy for several hours after a dose.

The result is a comforting glow and a deep sense of satisfaction. Any problems or stresses the user may have in his or her life seem very far away during this time, which can last for four or five hours. You may appear to be asleep, but actually be awake.[18]

As with opioid painkillers, though, people who go back for more are likely to find themselves developing dependencies on the drug: Their bodies will not manufacture dopamine without the heroin kick-start. Sam, a fifteen-year-old heroin addict, told the advocacy group Foundation for a Drug-Free World, "When you first shoot up, you will most likely puke and feel repelled, but soon you'll try it again. It will cling to you like an obsessed lover. The rush of the hit and the way you'll want more, as if you were being deprived of air—that's how it will trap you."[19]

The Crash

The heroin high may last three or four hours. Afterward the user comes down. Heroin users often call this phase *crashing*, and it is easy to see why. Soon after the effects of the drug wear off, the user may feel irritable or depressed. These ill feelings can be so pervasive that the user soon seeks to renew the high by ingesting more heroin.

A heroin high usually lasts three or four hours. As the high wears off, many users experience intense symptoms such as irritability or depression. This is referred to as crashing, *and it leads many users to seek out more heroin to avoid the crash.*

According to TheGoodDrugsGuide.com, it is not unusual for a heroin user to seek a new high within twenty-four hours of crashing from a previous high. During the crash there are often physical symptoms as well, including insomnia, muscle aches, and diarrhea. Finding a way to escape these physical effects gives the heroin user a reason to ingest another dose of the drug. Says TheGoodDrugsGuide.com,

> Since the drug affects the pleasure centers in the user's brain, their emotions may flat line in between times. After a time, the person may find that they don't have good feelings unless they are doing the heroin dance. In searching for a way to cope with or escape from negative feelings, they don't feel much of anything. The drug becomes the way for them to experience something positive in their lives.[20]

When taken in prescribed doses, in accordance with doctors' orders, opioid painkillers generally do not spark the interstellar highs or deep comedowns that most heroin users experience. Nevertheless, once patients start abusing the drugs—taking them in larger quantities than their doctors have prescribed as well as for longer periods—opioid painkillers are certainly capable of providing their own crashes.

British patient Cathryn Kemp found herself addicted to fentanyl after her release from the hospital in 2007 for treatment of pancreatitis, an inflammation of the pancreas. In 2008 she continued to take fentanyl tablets as a pain reliever, but after a breakup with a boyfriend she started relying on the opioid to ease her depression. Within a short time she was taking some thirty fentanyl tablets a day—and soon even more. She describes the crashes that afflicted her between pills:

> By the end of 2009 I had tried to cut down but the more I was taking the worse the withdrawal symptoms became.

"I would weep and laugh hysterically—I was convinced demons lived in my ceiling—and I could barely walk."[21]

—Cathryn Kemp, former fentanyl addict

At this stage I needed to have six every morning on waking just to stop the shaking and vomiting, since my body [absorbed] the previous day's dose overnight. I was taking forty-five lozenges throughout the day simply to keep these withdrawal symptoms at bay. I would weep and laugh hysterically—I was convinced demons lived in my ceiling—and I could barely walk.[21]

A Young Football Player's Story of Addiction

Growing up in the Seattle, Washington, suburb of Kitsap County, John Haskell lived and breathed football. By the age of thirteen, he already weighed 250 pounds (113 kg), large enough to play on the offensive and defensive lines on his middle school team. But John also sustained many injuries, including five concussions, and was living in constant pain.

His family doctor prescribed Vicodin. "I assumed it was perfectly fine," says John. "All I noticed was how the meds made me feel. There was no more pain going on." But John began relying too much on his Vicodin prescription to kill the pain, and he was soon addicted. "That high became all I cared about," he says. "Once I started, there was no turning back."

Within a year of beginning his Vicodin prescription, John moved on to heroin. John's parents missed the signs of his addiction. Their attention was focused mostly on the health of his mother, who suffered from multiple sclerosis, a debilitating illness that often leaves patients crippled. When he was sixteen, though, John's parents finally intervened and sent him to a drug rehabilitation program. John did emerge successfully from drug rehab.

But many teen addicts do not. "If teens are introduced at such a young age to powerful prescription drugs like Vicodin, you're only going to see damaging effects," says Jamison Monroe, director of Newport Academy, the drug treatment facility in California that treated John. "And the younger the person is, the more likely they are to become addicts."

Quoted in Blake Wyman, "Is Your Teen Addicted to Painkillers? I Was, Says Former Football Star," *Hamilton Spectator* (Ontario, Canada), April 24, 2017. www.thespec.com.

Military Veterans and Opioids

Among the people whose experiences mirror those of Kemp's are tens of thousands of US veterans. According to the US Department of Veterans Affairs (VA), which provides medical care for former members of the military, some 60 percent of veterans of the wars in Afghanistan and Iraq returned home complaining of chronic pain—a staggering number, considering that more than 2 million Americans served in the two wars. And for years, VA doctors responded to their needs by prescribing opioid painkillers.

Bryan McDonel of Pine Bluff, Arkansas, served two tours in Iraq and one tour in Afghanistan. Before his second deployment to Iraq, McDonel was injured at home when he was struck in the back by a trailer hitch. He underwent surgery, then returned to his unit in time to deploy to Iraq a second time. Thinking back, McDonel says, it was probably a mistake to return to Iraq because his back had not yet fully healed. "We knew the deployment was coming up, and I didn't want to let my team down," McDonel says. "You know that whole, 'I'm not gonna get left behind.' I was hard-headed. I ended up probably reinjuring it before it had time to heal."[22]

McDonel says he endured his second tour in Iraq mostly by swallowing doses of Vicodin pills, taking six pills a day—which his doctor had prescribed. When he returned home, he continued to take Vicodin to deal with his chronic pain.

And then he deployed for Afghanistan but failed to take enough Vicodin pills. After several days of duty in Afghanistan, McDonel ran out of pills. He soon started feeling ill. "My lower back hurt like hell," he says. "And I thought I'd hurt myself again, but then I started feeling real sick. I didn't want to get out of the bed, and I didn't understand what that was."[23] McDonel saw an Army medic, who advised him that he had not reinjured his back but was likely suffering from the withdrawal effects of suddenly cutting off his Vicodin supply. The medic solved that problem by giving him a bottle of Percocet pills. McDonel returned home following his deployment to Afghanistan, thoroughly addicted to opioids.

> "My lower back hurt like hell. And I thought I'd hurt myself again, but then I started feeling real sick. I didn't want to get out of the bed, and I didn't understand what that was."[23]
>
> —Bryan McDonel, US Army veteran and opioid addict

A US army soldier is helped after being injured by an improvised explosive device in Afghanistan. Many US military personnel get injured while on active duty. It is estimated that 650,000 veterans of the Iraq and Afghanistan wars rely on opioid painkillers to treat their pain.

After returning home he found a job as an instructor for the Arkansas National Guard, but his opioid addiction soon dominated his life. He was unable to function in the job and in 2011 had to resign. His marriage fell apart; he lost his home and was forced to live out of his car. To find enough opioids to satisfy his addiction, McDonel has often turned to drug dealers. "It's been one day at a time," McDonel says of his opioid addiction. "Looking daily to find work, every day, working hard to try and start relationships again."[24] According to the VA, McDonel is among some 650,000 veterans of Iraq and Afghanistan who rely on opioid painkillers.

Young Opioid Abusers

Veterans (and most other adults) who develop opioid addictions often start down that road after receiving prescriptions from their physicians. While some young people also get addicted to painkillers this way, many are just looking for quick highs and, often, they need venture no further than home to find what they are looking for. Young people often find prescription pain pills right in their own homes. A 2017 study by the Johns Hopkins Bloomberg School of Public Health in Baltimore, Maryland, found that 70 percent of parents who take opioid painkillers do not bother to lock them up or to secure them in any way. This means that young people have easy access to their parents' pills. "We can't leave opioids just sitting on the nightstand or kitchen counter," says Eileen McDonald, a faculty member at Hopkins Bloomberg. "Parents need to be at a minimum putting them out of the way, but ideally putting them under lock and key."[25]

A similar 2017 study, conducted by the Central Ohio Poison Control Center, found that in 2015 poison control centers in America received eleven thousand calls reporting cases in which young people had ingested opioid painkillers. The study said about half of those calls reported the drugs were taken accidentally while the other half reported that the youths had intentionally swallowed the drugs.

Opioid addiction among youth has become a global problem. One young victim of opioid abuse was sixteen-year-old Michael Cornacchia from the Irish town of Cork, who was found dead in his home in January 2017 after ingesting a lethal dose of an opioid painkiller. "I was shocked when I woke up this morning and saw the ambulance coming," said the Cornacchia family's next-door neighbor, Thomas O'Mahony. "One of my sons used to hang around with him and every summer we would go over to the field playing soccer. He was a lovely soccer player and a nice young fella."[26]

Michael Cornacchia's death illustrates that many victims of opioid overdose do not take painkillers for the purposes for which they are prescribed by doctors but, rather, to achieve narcotic highs. Indeed, as his neighbor described him, Cornacchia was a vibrant, healthy, and athletic teen who had no reason to seek relief from the deep and unceasing pain opioid drugs are intended to provide.

CHAPTER THREE

Living in the Grasp of Opioids

Visitors to Philadelphia often tour such historical sites as Independence Hall, the Liberty Bell, and the Betsy Ross House. Just a few miles away from these landmarks of American history is an area of the city not too many outsiders take the time to visit. In the city's hardscrabble Kensington neighborhood, a community of heroin addicts has emerged alongside a stretch of railroad tracks. Approaching the scene, reporters for the *Philadelphia Inquirer* wrote, "Tens of thousands of used syringes and their tossed-off orange caps cover the sloping ground like a plague of locusts. The contaminated needles make conditions so hazardous that even some police officers are reluctant to traverse the embankments to get to the dead overdose victims at the bottom." In fact, death by overdose is a common sight in the vicinity. "Addicts—many with needle marks so fresh that still-drying blood glistens in the sun—twist their bodies into unnatural forms to crouch and teeter on the trash-covered banks as they shoot up," the newspaper reported. "Others sleep under nearby bridges or in makeshift shelters surrounded by garbage, drugs, and death."[27]

Police estimate that about a hundred heroin addicts live along the railroad tracks, although their numbers rise and fall daily. In a city that endures some nine hundred drug overdose deaths per year, police believe a significant number of the victims lose their lives along the tracks in Kensington. Proof of the area's high mortality rate can be found underfoot: Police estimate that no fewer than a half-million used syringes are strewn about the area. "I questioned whether I was still in the US," said agent Gary Tuggle of the US Drug Enforcement Administration (DEA) after visiting the area. "It's like a third-world country."[28]

Lives Ruined by Opioids

For the people who live along the railroad tracks in Philadelphia's Kensington neighborhood, procuring and using heroin has become their sole purpose in life. Schoolwork, jobs, fun activities, and friends all become secondary as the addicts relentlessly pursue their next heroin highs. For people addicted to opioid painkillers, finding and using drugs often becomes the only purpose in their lives as well.

Moreover, finding money to pay for the drugs becomes an all-consuming mission. In big cities, addicts are known to commit petty crimes or turn to prostitution to support their habits. In the suburbs and in small towns, addicts may steal from family members or friends. For many people, addictions to opioids have cost them their savings, careers, and families.

Used needles litter the ground along the train tracks in Philadelphia's Kensington neighborhood, which has become known as a community for heroin addicts. Police estimate that as many as ten thousand needles are strewn around the stretch of train tracks at any given time.

Frank Huntley knows the ruination of opioid addiction first-hand. Huntley built a successful house painting business in Worcester, Massachusetts. In 1998 he suffered a shoulder injury, which led to two surgeries—and considerable pain. To ease the pain so that he could continue painting for a living, his doctor provided him with a relatively minor prescription for Percocet—10 milligram pills, to be taken twice a day.

Eventually, his doctor grew concerned about the prescription after learning that long-term use of Percocet could damage the liver. "My doctor called me one day. I was working and I was still hurt," Huntley says. "He says, 'Frank, I want to stop Percocet and start a new drug called OxyContin, it just came out. Percocet is going to eat your liver. This is a time capsule and you only have to take a couple a day because it will last like 12 hours.' So that's how we started."[29]

Soon, Huntley was addicted to Oxy-Contin. Eventually, he built up a tolerance to OxyContin but still experienced pain. So his doctor prescribed a second opioid, methadone. "So then I was on Oxy in the morning and methadone at night,"[30] he says.

Opioids were now controlling his life. By 2004 Huntley's business was gone—he was unable to work as he constantly struggled to feed his opioid habit. His wife divorced him and moved out of their home, taking the couple's daughter with her. Unable to earn a living, Huntley lost his home and was forced to move in with his mother. He rarely saw his daughter. Over the next eight years he drifted from doctor to doctor, convincing some physicians to write new prescriptions for pain pills. At the height of his addiction, Huntley consumed the equivalent of 90 milligrams of OxyContin three or four times a day in addition to methadone pills he took as well. "This medicine made me tired, made me moody, made me sick, oh my God, sick," he says. Huntley finally entered drug rehabilitation in 2012. He says, "[Opioids] suck your brain away. They suck everything away. I had everything. My company was going big. I had everything with my ex-wife. It was amazing. And it just went away. I was weak, I was in pain."[31]

> "I had everything. My company was going big. I had everything with my ex-wife. It was amazing. And it just went away. I was weak, I was in pain."[31]
>
> —Frank Huntley, former OxyContin addict

33

Finding Drugs at Home

Huntley's addiction to opioid painkillers started after he sustained an on-the-job injury. For many people, addictions begin much earlier in life. Many addicts start using opioids as teenagers. They experiment with the drugs after finding their parents' prescriptions in medicine cabinets at home. A recent study by the advocacy group Partnership for Drug-Free Kids found that 42 percent of teens who abuse drugs have consumed pills prescribed to their parents. Marcel Casavant, coauthor of a 2017 study on opioid abuse among young people for the Johns Hopkins Bloomberg Center, adds, "The opioid crisis which has been affecting our adult population has now trickled down to our children. When adults bring these medications into their homes, they can become a danger to the children that live there."[32]

Opioid-Induced Constipation

Virtually all opioid users, whether addicts or short-term users following a doctor's orders, develop severe bouts of constipation. Just as there are opioid receptors in the brain, there are also opioid receptors in the gastrointestinal tract. Unlike the brain, the gastrointestinal tract does not produce dopamine. Instead, opioids spark a much different effect when they bind with the receptors in the gut. Essentially, they slow things down—meaning digested food moves slowly through the bowels, causing constipation. The condition is known as opioid-induced constipation (OIC).

Most cases of constipation can be cured by drinking fluids and eating foods high in fiber, such as fruits and vegetables. But these common cures often do not work with people who consume opioids because the opioid receptors in the bowels slow everything down, regardless of the fiber content of the food that was consumed.

The legendary rock-and-roll star Elvis Presley is believed to have suffered from OIC so severely that it contributed to his death. Presley, whose body was found in a bathroom in his Memphis mansion, died in 1977. An autopsy revealed the level of codeine in his body was ten times normal therapeutic levels. The autopsy also revealed that Presley's colon was six inches in diameter—the diameter of the normal adult colon is no more than two inches. Evidently, the singer died from heart failure during an unsuccessful attempt to move his bowels.

That's how Kirby Kraus of Wasilla, Alaska, first started abusing drugs. At the age of twelve, he found his parents' prescriptions in a medicine cabinet at home. Within a short time, after experimenting with Vicodin, Percocet, and OxyContin, he moved on to heroin. Soon, he was living on the streets, sleeping on benches in Wasilla's Nunley Park. "The only solution I knew was putting a needle in my arm,"[33] says Kraus, who eventually stopped using opioids after completing a drug rehabilitation program.

Another young user was eighteen-year-old high school wrestler Drew Gintis, who started taking opioids after he was injured. Soon, the athlete from Cary, North Carolina, was addicted. When his prescription ran out, he stole pills from medicine cabinets of friends and relatives and then moved on to heroin. Drew won an athletic scholarship to college, but he never enrolled. Instead, his parents urged him to enter a drug treatment program. "I knew he was having problems," says Drew's mother, Marsha Gintis. "It was really, really tough. He started not going to school. He had gotten into every college he wanted to get into. But by the end of his senior year it was clear he wasn't going to college. He had changed. He was angry."[34]

Drew entered a drug rehab program, but it did not work. He dropped out of rehab, then spent time living in homeless shelters. Finally, he moved to Florida to live with a friend. Drew found a job and seemed to have straightened out his life, but when his parents drove to Florida to meet him for dinner, Drew never showed up. The next day, police reported that Drew died from a fentanyl overdose.

Increasing the Opioid High

Addicts like Drew Gintis and Kirby Kraus were relentless in their pursuits of the highs achieved through opioids—finding drugs first in medicine cabinets then buying them illegally on the streets. Sometimes, the illegal trade in opioids reflects the degree of desperation faced by addicts to obtain the drugs they need. One such method involves the painkiller fentanyl, which is often administered in the form of an adhesive patch. The patch, treated with the drug, is applied topically to the skin. The opioid is then absorbed by the blood and carried to the brain.

The patch is designed to remain in place for seventy-two hours, meaning that the patch serves as a time-release mechanism. Over the course of three days, the fentanyl is slowly released into the body, giving the patient extended relief that lasts well beyond the few hours of relief provided by most opioid pills. When the patch is exhausted, the patient is expected to discard the patch, but police have often found that drug addicts obtain the used patches—possibly buying them from patients. The fabric in the used patches continues to contain remnants of the drug, and addicts have found they can ingest the remaining fentanyl content by chewing the patches.

Other addicts try to boost their highs by using what are known as "potentiators," substances that heighten the narcotic effect of the opioid. As far back as the 1800s, when morphine was first developed, patients found they could increase the pain-killing effects of the drug by consuming whiskey or other alcoholic beverages. Alcohol is a sedative, meaning it can have a sluggish effect on the drinker. By combining opioids with alcohol, the user will at first experience a feeling of euphoria, but that feeling is soon followed by drowsiness, mental confusion, poor memory and concentration, numbness, anxiety, intense sluggishness, and depressed breathing.

There are numerous other potentiators—including some that may at first seem quite harmless. Grapefruit juice is widely available in grocery stores, but patients are warned by their doctors not to consume opioids with the beverage. The reason: The body contains chemicals, known as enzymes, that break down foods and medications as they are consumed, enabling the body to absorb them. Grapefruit juice—and other citrus juices—contain chemicals known as furanocoumarins that block those enzymes. In other words, people who consume grapefruit juice have a more difficult time absorbing and breaking down food and medicine.

In most cases, the effects are mild—by no means is grapefruit juice a harmful product. But people who take medications are advised by their doctors not to consume the pills with a glass of grapefruit juice. Doctors want the pills to be absorbed, and broken down by the body, naturally. If opioids are consumed with grapefruit juice, the pills are absorbed by the body more slowly. That means the high lasts longer. "Taking one tablet with a glass

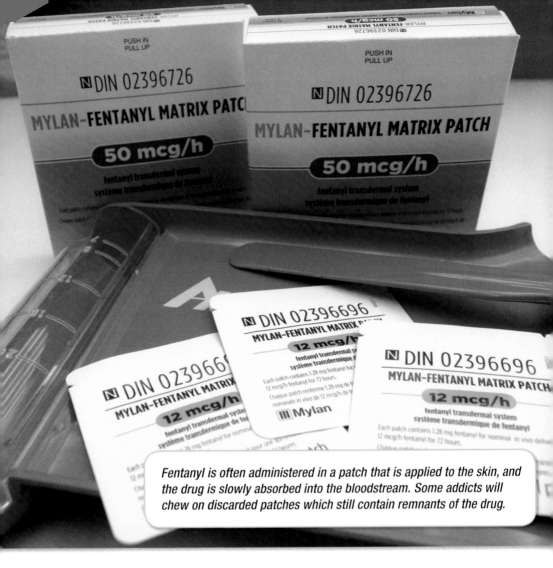

Fentanyl is often administered in a patch that is applied to the skin, and the drug is slowly absorbed into the bloodstream. Some addicts will chew on discarded patches which still contain remnants of the drug.

of grapefruit juice is like taking 20 tablets with a glass of water,"[35] says biologist David Bailey, a researcher at the Lawson Health Research Institute in London, Ontario. Over time, many addicts have learned these and other techniques for increasing and lengthening the opioid high. The pleasurable effect is fleeting, however, as their bodies begin to experience drug overdoses.

Side Effects of Opioid Abuse

Regardless of how long the high lasts, addicts often experience a whole array of unpleasant and dangerous side effects from the drugs. Among the most common are drowsiness, confusion, widespread itching (a condition known as pruritus), and nausea.

In men, opioid abuse also leads to a decrease in the hormone testosterone—and a lack of testosterone causes erectile dysfunction.

Short-term memory loss is another side effect of opioid abuse. In 1997 a doctor issued a Vicodin prescription to TV star Matthew Perry to help relieve pain caused by injuries the actor suffered in a jet ski accident. But after his injuries healed, Perry found himself hooked on Vicodin, and he kept taking the pills. "I used to have a little bit of a Vicodin problem," Perry says, "and when I say 'a little bit' I mean I used to take enough on a daily basis to kill a baby elephant."[36] Perry acknowledged taking dozens of pills a day over the course of a four-year addiction to the drug.

During that period Perry was a star of the hit TV show *Friends*. Perry says a lot of the work he did on the show remains a blur due to the short-term memory loss he suffered while taking Vicodin. Perry says he was able to deliver his lines on the show, but after the taping of an episode concluded the actor had no memory of what he had just done. "I don't remember three years of [*Friends*]. . . . I was a little out of it at the time,"[37] he says.

> "I used to have a little bit of a Vicodin problem, and when I say 'a little bit' I mean I used to take enough on a daily basis to kill a baby elephant."[36]
>
> —Matthew Perry, TV actor

Opioid Overdoses

While a lack of testosterone, annoying itching, and memory loss can be unpleasant, the most dangerous side effect of opioids is their impact on the respiratory system. Opioids slow down the body's respiratory system—making breathing slower. People who take their opioid pain medications in properly prescribed doses may notice their breathing slowing, but it is rarely harmful to them. However, when people overdose on opioid painkillers or heroin, they may lapse into the condition known as respiratory depression. In other words, they take too few breaths to maintain the functions of their vital organs. Frequently, the result of respiratory depression caused by opioid overdose is death.

In March 2017 the four children of airline pilot Brian Halye and his wife, Courtney, woke up one morning in their Centerville, Ohio,

Many addicts experience uncomfortable and dangerous side effects from opioid use. The most common are drowsiness, nausea, and severe itching.

home to find the bodies of their parents. Overnight, Brian and Courtney had both suffered fatal overdoses of fentanyl. Evidence gathered by police at the scene suggested the Halyes had both been addicted to opioids for years. "I just woke up and my two parents are on the floor," the couple's thirteen-year-old son told a 911 dispatcher. "My sister said they're not waking up. They're not breathing."[38]

Chewing OxyContin

For years, addicts found they could obtain heroin-like highs by chewing OxyContin pills. When the drug was introduced in 1995, its manufacturer, Purdue Pharma, built a time-release mechanism into the pills, enabling the drug's effects to last up to twelve hours. Addicts found they could defeat the time-release mechanism, and receive the drug's entire hit all at once, by chewing the pills, releasing the opioid in full force. "It's better than heroin. It's more pure. It's like no other feeling I had before," said Jason Fisher, a former heroin addict who explained the rush he received by chewing OxyContin pills.

Word of the effectiveness of chewing OxyContin spread quickly. Purdue Pharma responded to reports of the abuse of the drug, but it took until 2010 for the pharmaceutical company to find a way to prevent abusers from defeating the time-release feature. When chewed, the new version of the drug cannot be ground into a powder; instead, the pill breaks into chunks that maintain the time-release feature.

Even though OxyContin is now tamper proof, many narcotics experts believe the damage has been done. John Burke, president of the National Association of Drug Diversion Investigators, says when addicts found they could no longer get their highs by chewing the pills, they sought their highs elsewhere—turning to other opioid painkillers or heroin. "It's just a matter of switching," he says. "If I'm an addict, I'm going to find a drug that works."

Quoted in Hal Marcovitz, "Witness: Oxycontin 'Better than Heroin,'" *Morning Call* (Allentown, PA), April 6, 2002. www.mcall.com.

Quoted in Abby Goodnough and Katie Zezima, "Drug Is Harder to Abuse, but Users Persevere," *New York Times*, June 15, 2011. www.nytimes.com.

Lying to Their Doctors

Despite the consequences of abusing opioids, addicts relentlessly pursue their next highs. One tactic used by addicts to obtain drugs is to lie to their doctors, claiming their pain persists well after their injuries heal. Cathryn Kemp, the British woman who consumed as many as forty-five fentanyl pills per day during the throes of her addiction, admits to lying to her doctor to procure her prescriptions. "He knew I was becoming dependent but my fear of coming off them and living without pain relief meant that I kept persuading him to give me more, pleading, manipulating and lying, to get an increased dose,"[39] she says.

Doctors sometimes find it difficult to know whether a patient is addicted to painkillers. Says Washington, DC, physician Kenneth Lin, "I've had patients I trusted turn out to be junkies in need of a fix. An earnest, well-dressed young man once came to my office complaining of a common chronic condition that, he said, had not been relieved by high doses of over-the-counter painkillers. He convinced me to prescribe him narcotic pills."[40] Lin says over the course of a year the patient returned for subsequent appointments and always gave him compelling reasons to renew his opioid prescriptions.

> "I've had patients I trusted turn out to be junkies in need of a fix."[40]
>
> —Kenneth Lin, physician

But then the patient was treated in a hospital emergency room for a drug overdose. At that point, physicians determined the patient had obtained, and had been using, opioid prescriptions from three different physicians, including Lin.

Doctor Shopping

Not only did the patient lie to Lin about the level of his pain, but he told the same lies to two other doctors. The patient who obtained prescriptions from Lin as well as the other physicians had engaged in the practice of "doctor shopping" or "doctor hopping." In other words, a patient sees a doctor to report a painful condition and obtain a prescription for opioid painkillers and then, after obtaining the prescription, schedules an appointment with another doctor to report the same condition and obtain a second prescription. And, as Lin's case illustrates, the patient found a third doctor willing to write a prescription. In fact, a recent study published in the medical journal *PLOS ONE* estimated that some 4 million opioid prescriptions a year are obtained by patients who get them from multiple doctors.

In addition to doctor shopping, addicts often resort to other forms of subterfuge, altering their doctors' prescriptions to obtain more pills than have been prescribed. The journal *Pain Medicine* cited a case in which a patient presented a prescription to a pharmacist in which the doctor had approved one hundred pills for the man. The pharmacist thought something was off and contacted the doctor to verify the prescription. It turned out the doctor had prescribed just ten pills for the patient, but the patient added an extra zero to the prescription himself. In fact, after checking their records, the doctor and pharmacist discovered the patient pulled the same stunt the month before—and got away with it.

Other patients rely on hospital emergency rooms for their pills. Under law, no hospital emergency room can turn away a patient. Therefore, patients have been known to roam from ER to ER, where they are often able to convince the emergency room doctors they are in pain and in need of opioid painkillers. After receiving their prescriptions, the patients move on to the next ER.

As the cases of Kirby Kraus and Drew Gintis illustrate, addiction to opioids can start at a young age. In Drew's case, his addiction cost him a college scholarship, and ultimately, his life. Even if opioid users survive their addictions, they may often lose their homes, livelihoods, and families—an outcome suffered by Frank Huntley. Of course, many heroin addicts end up homeless, resorting to theft or prostitution to obtain the money they need to feed their habits. Sadly, as the situation in Philadelphia illustrates, their lives often end in forgotten urban enclaves as other addicts step over their bodies seeking their next highs.

CHAPTER FOUR

Regulating Opioids

A 2016 poll conducted by the Kaiser Family Foundation sought to gauge what people who live with pain think about the opioid painkillers they take. The response by patients was overwhelmingly supportive of their medications. A total of 92 percent of the patients surveyed by the foundation said their opioid prescriptions are effective in reducing their pain. Moreover, 57 percent of the patients said their quality of life had improved since they started their prescriptions. "All you hear about in the news are the ones who overdose or abuse their prescriptions," says Sandra Gartz, a sixty-two-year-old Kitchener, Ontario, woman, who for many years has taken codeine for fibromyalgia, a disease that causes pain in the muscles and bones. "You don't hear about people like me . . . I never got addicted to it. I have always taken it as prescribed."[41]

The beliefs aired by Gartz and many other opioid painkiller users reflect the quandary faced by physicians and government officials: How do they ensure that people in pain still have access to opioid painkillers while also taking steps to reduce abuse and addiction? Says Joshua Landau, a Greensboro, North Carolina, surgeon, "As a physician, I grapple daily with the opioid abuse epidemic plaguing our state and nation. I weigh my responsibility to my patients' well-being and to the larger community. . . .The key question is how to ensure safe use of a substance intended to relieve suffering, but with the potential for abuse and harm."[42]

CDC Issues Opioid Guidelines

In fact, as opioid abuse has grown into a national health emergency, the federal government as well as many state governments have undertaken a number of initiatives to combat opioid painkiller addiction. In 2013 the US Food and Drug Administration (FDA), which regulates prescription drugs in America, required the makers of extended-release opioid painkillers, such as OxyContin, to include so-called black-box warnings on pill bottle labels. The warnings, which are printed on black backgrounds, include statements alerting users of the potential for abuse. In 2016 the FDA extended the requirement for black-box warnings to all opioid painkillers.

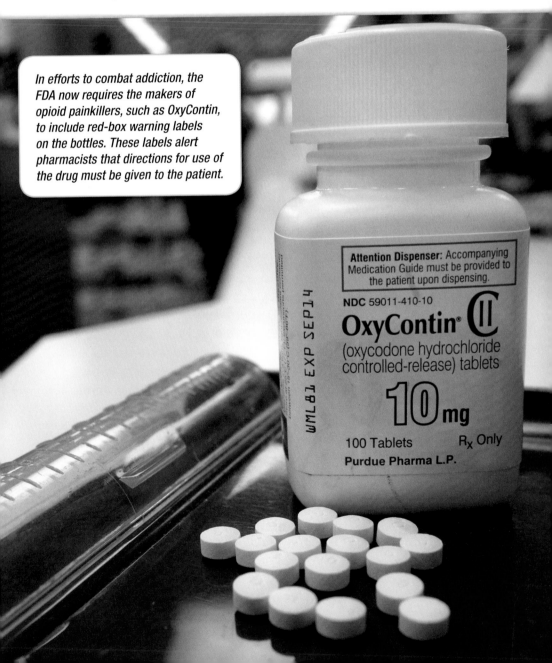

In efforts to combat addiction, the FDA now requires the makers of opioid painkillers, such as OxyContin, to include red-box warning labels on the bottles. These labels alert pharmacists that directions for use of the drug must be given to the patient.

Moreover, in March 2017 the CDC issued new guidelines to physicians, recommending how opioid drugs should be prescribed to patients. For cases that fall under what is known as "palliative care," meaning care provided to patients who are not expected to recover from their illnesses, the CDC said doctors should continue prescribing opioid painkillers. But for everyone else, the CDC recommended that opioid painkillers be prescribed only after all other methods of reducing pain have failed. Moreover, the CDC said, if doctors find it necessary to prescribe opioid painkillers to reduce their patients' pain, they would do well to prescribe minimal doses for short periods of time only. "Don't use opioids routinely for chronic pain," the CDC advised doctors. "When opioids are used, prescribe the lowest possible effective dosage. . . . Only provide the quantity needed for the expected duration of pain."[43]

The CDC called on doctors and their patients to accept other methods of pain reduction, such as non-opioid painkillers—including such over-the-counter products as Tylenol, Motrin, and Advil—as well as physical therapy or lifestyle changes. For example, the CDC suggested, if a patient is suffering from chronic knee pain, it may be a better idea for the patient to lose weight than to swallow opioid painkillers to dull the pain. "We don't want people getting more opioids than needed," says Debra Houry, director of the CDC's National Center for Injury Prevention and Control. "We want people to have a proper course of treatment, but still want patients and health care providers to use caution."[44]

Eliminating Doctor Hopping

While the CDC has concentrated on changing how doctors prescribe opioid painkillers, state governments have focused their attention largely on cutting down on ways in which drug abusers gain access to the pills. For example, to eliminate the practice of doctor hopping, state governments have enacted laws prohibiting patients from obtaining prescription opioid painkillers from more than one physician. To enforce the laws, the states have created patient databases: when a physician writes a prescription for an opioid painkiller, the patient's name is entered into the database.

To eliminate the practice of "doctor hopping," state governments have created patient databases. If the patient's name is already in the database, the doctor is prohibited from prescribing the patient an additional prescription for opioid pain medication.

If a patient shows up at another doctor's office seeking an opioid prescription, the doctor is required to check the database. If the patient's name has already been entered in the database, the second doctor is prohibited from writing an opioid prescription for the patient. Only the original doctor can continue writing opioid prescriptions for that patient.

Kentucky became the first state to enact an opioid database in 2012. Since then, another forty-eight states have established similar databases—by 2017, only Georgia had failed to establish a database. However, lawmakers in Georgia had prepared legislation to create an opioid database for their state and were confident the legislation would be adopted. "What it does is prevent doctor hopping," says Renee Unterman, a Georgia state senator who authored the legislation creating the database. Unterman suggests that in addition to preventing patients from doctor hopping, the state's database would help keep opioid drugs out of the illegal trade. "It prevents these legal drugs from becoming street drugs and sold at exorbitant prices,"[45] she asserts.

Limiting Pills to Patients

But even patients who don't attempt to obtain prescriptions from multiple doctors or through illegal channels are finding their access to opioids falling under new limitations. Some states have enacted laws limiting the number of pills that can be obtained with a single prescription: by early 2017, ten states—Massachusetts, New York, Pennsylvania, Connecticut, Rhode Island, Vermont, New Hampshire, New Jersey, Maine, and Arizona—had enacted laws limiting the number of pills that can be included in opioid pain prescriptions.

In March 2016 Massachusetts became the first state to enact such a law when state legislators limited patients to supplies lasting no more than seven days. After the initial seven-day supply runs out, patients must return to their physicians for new prescriptions. Moreover, the law limits a patient under the age of eighteen to receiving no more than a single seven-day prescription for opioid painkillers. "When you see a state legislature or governor or attorney general put forward this type of intervention, what it demonstrates is an understanding of what's been fueling the opioid crisis," says Andrew Kolodny, the director of the Opioid Policy Research Collaborative at Brandeis University in Massachusetts. "Until very recently, which is why I think the epidemic has worsened . . . policymakers didn't understand that over-prescribing was fueling the problem."[46]

> "Until very recently, which is why I think the epidemic has worsened . . . policymakers didn't understand that over-prescribing was fueling the problem."[46]
>
> —Andrew Kolodny, physician and addiction treatment specialist

Some states have enacted even stricter laws. In 2017 New Jersey lawmakers enacted a five-day limit on opioid prescriptions. Kolodny endorsed the New Jersey law. "If you supply someone with a thirty-day supply when they need only two pills, the rest are in the medicine chest where they're a hazard," he says. "We do need much more cautious prescribing."[47]

Doctors Oppose Opioid Restrictions

Laws such as those adopted in Massachusetts and New Jersey, as well as the actions by the federal government to persuade doctors to change their policies regarding opioids, have been met with harsh reactions from many physicians who believe doctors—and not the government—should decide how many pills to prescribe to their patients. "I have a patient with inoperable spinal stenosis who needs to be able to keep chopping wood to heat his home," says Robert L. Wergin, a physician in rural Milford, Nebraska. "A one-size-fits-all prescription algorithm just doesn't fit him."[48] (Spinal stenosis is a degenerative and painful condition of the spine in which the spinal canal narrows, causing bones within the spinal cord to pinch the surrounding tissue.)

> "I have a patient with inoperable spinal stenosis who needs to be able to keep chopping wood to heat his home. A one-size-fits-all prescription algorithm just doesn't fit him."[48]
>
> —Robert L. Wergin, Nebraska physician

Instead, the American Medical Association (AMA) Task Force to Reduce Opioid Addiction has called on physicians to become better schooled in the dangers of overprescribing the medications. "If—in my clinical judgment—based on my education and training I believe that a medication will not be helpful, I will tell my patient 'no,'" says Patrice Harris, chairperson of the AMA's Opioid Task Force. "Our prescribing decisions must be judicious, deliberative, and rooted in the art and science of medicine."[49]

Moreover, the AMA Task Force also called on states to improve their opioid databases. One drawback among the databases, critics point out, is that they are not linked—meaning that somebody whose name can be found in a database in one state can easily drive to a neighboring state, show up in a hospital emergency room complaining of pain, and receive an opioid prescription. Says Stuart Gitlow, president of the American Society of Addiction Medicine, "I'm based in Rhode Island, for instance, but a patient could easily drive to Connecticut, Massachusetts, Vermont, or New Hampshire in no time at all and get multiple other prescriptions. The more you look at it, the more you realize there are holes in the system."[50]

Increasing Access to Opioids in Europe

As the United States and Canada tighten restrictions on opioid painkillers, efforts are underway to increase access to the drugs in parts of Europe. A study of opioid use in a dozen European countries found that regulations on opioid prescriptions are so stringent that the drugs are now virtually impossible to obtain. Even patients suffering the most severe and painful conditions, such as cancer, have little access to opioids. The study, done by the group Access to Opioid Medication in Europe (ATOME), focused on Estonia, Latvia, Lithuania, Poland, Slovakia, Hungary, Slovenia, Serbia, Bulgaria, Greece, Cyprus, and Turkey. It was commissioned by the European Union Seventh Framework Programme, which studies public health issues for European Union member countries.

ATOME has launched a campaign to help ease restrictions on opioid prescriptions in those countries. Says Shelia Payne, a coauthor of the report and professor at the International Observatory on End of Life Care at Lancaster University in Great Britain, "Opioids are treated as narcotics and very strictly controlled because there is a fear that opioids will cause addiction. But if they are used at the end of life or if people are in great pain, addiction is not a problem. In some countries, you can only get opioids if you are in hospital, which is no good if you wish to die at home."

Quoted in National Pain Report, "Access to Opioids in Europe Called 'Human Right,'" January 16, 2015. http://nationalpainreport.com.

Pain Unlike Other Ailments

Wergin and other doctors point out that pain is unlike other ailments that inflict the body because it is not easy to diagnose. Certainly, a doctor looking at an X-ray revealing a broken wrist knows the patient must be in pain—but how much pain? To help them decide their patients' levels of pain doctors often ask the patients to rate their pain levels on a scale of 0 to 10, with 0 reflecting no pain and 10 the most intense and unbearable pain.

But some patients endure pain better than others—pain that one patient might describe at level 5 may feel like level 10 to another patient. Says psychiatrist Jay Tracy, "Pain may be difficult to diagnose clearly and is lacking in explanation. Not only is it difficult for the physician to accurately diagnose and explain, it is difficult for [patients] to understand exactly what is going on. . . . Pain can last a long time. It can last beyond the normal time it takes for a healing. This pain is not only difficult to understand but it is also difficult to treat."[51]

Chronic pain may be hardest to gauge. Only the arthritis patient truly knows how much discomfort the condition is causing. Wergin, among other doctors, does not strive to ensure patients are pain free, but rather, that they are able to achieve realistic goals. He wants to help them return to their jobs, walk, and perform other routine tasks for themselves, and be able to get a good night's sleep. Therefore, many physicians do not believe the

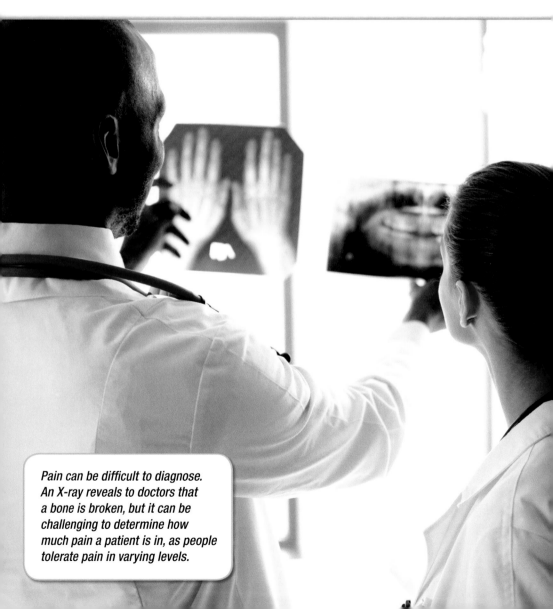

Pain can be difficult to diagnose. An X-ray reveals to doctors that a bone is broken, but it can be challenging to determine how much pain a patient is in, as people tolerate pain in varying levels.

government should be in a position to tell them how to treat their patients' pain. Instead, they maintain that their education, experience, and personal knowledge of their patients' cases should drive their decisions on how to medicate their patients.

Enduring Patient Misbehavior

Some doctors believe so strongly in their treatment methods—including the use of opioids to treat pain—that they are willing to endure misbehavior by their patients. Many doctors acknowledge that some patients may be willing to lie or even commit crimes to obtain more pills than they have been prescribed, but they also realize that pain often causes some people to act irrationally.

Norleena Gullett, a physician who treats cancer patients at the Simon Cancer Center at Indiana University, recalls a case in which one of her patients altered a prescription in which Gullet approved her for thirty Percocet pills. The patient changed the number of pills to ninety. The forgery was discovered—the patient was arrested and jailed for four days. After the patient was released from jail, she returned to Gullett's office for a follow-up appointment and told Gullett that she was still in pain. Says Gullett:

> Do I think my patient was abusing Percocet? Maybe, but the answer isn't quite that easy. Maybe she had more pain and was afraid to tell us. Maybe we had unconsciously communicated that her pain should have been well-controlled with the drugs we gave her. Or maybe she was selling the extra pills to help pay for her treatment.
>
> So what was I to do when she returned for radiation treatment after her release from jail? She still had cancer, still had pain. . . . Most important, she was still my patient.[52]

Gullett says she found herself with little choice: She wrote a new prescription for Percocet for her patient. She says, "While prescription drug abuse is a problem and needs to be recognized, the reasons doctors prescribe painkillers should not be forgotten."[53]

Banning Opioids for Poor People

Some doctors worry that the patients most likely to be affected by government restrictions on opioids are those who need government assistance to obtain their prescriptions. Starting in 2017, for example, the province of Ontario, Canada, banned opioid painkillers from the Ontario Drug Benefit, a government-sponsored program that helps low-income people and others afford prescription drugs. The ban was aimed at keeping the drugs out of the hands of drug dealers—or, at least, ensuring that the provincial government does not help pay for the opioid painkillers obtained by drug dealers.

Administrators banned opioids from the program's approved list of drugs after determining that physicians in Ontario wrote 8.1 million prescriptions for opioids in 2015. That amounts to roughly one prescription for every resident of the province between the ages of fifteen and sixty-four. Advocates for eliminating opioids from the Ontario Drug Benefit contend that many people who are enrolled in the program use them for illegal purposes—many selling the drugs to others. Or, officials contend, many users return to their doctors, convincing the physicians to write new prescriptions after falsely claiming their original prescriptions were lost or stolen. "By far the vast majority of people who want these drugs are using them for illicit purposes,"[54] insisted physician Gordon Jones, head of the emergency department at Kingston General Hospital in Ontario.

But opponents of the ban point out that a significant number of patients who obtain their prescriptions through the program are legitimately in need of opioid painkillers. A 2016 study found that at least 20 percent of the patients who are enrolled in the Ontario Drug Benefit have been prescribed opioid painkillers by their physicians.

Some medical professionals insist that Ontario's ban will probably have little effect on the illegal drug trade. Rather, they predict, the ban will serve mostly to deny pain-killing medications to poor people who suffer pain—and these patients will then be very likely to seek their opioids through illegal channels. "The solution of tightening down prescription guidelines might affect 5 percent of those who take opioid medications, if that," says David Walton, a professor at the Western University School of Physical Therapy

Will Regulating Opioid Painkillers Lead to Heroin Use?

Addiction experts have long believed that prescription opioid painkillers can serve as gateway drugs to heroin. Richard Taite, a Malibu, California, addictions counselor, points to statistics compiled by the National Survey on Drug Use and Health indicating that heroin use grew from 373,000 Americans in 2007 to some 669,000 in 2012. "Individuals who regularly use opioid . . . medications do not often recognize that they are using a medication that can be a gateway to heroin use," says Taite.

In 2016 a study published in the *New England Journal of Medicine* focused on whether new state and federal regulations reducing people's access to opioid painkillers could lead those patients to use heroin. The study concluded that new laws and regulations have little impact on whether people transition from opioid painkillers to heroin. According to the study, people who are likely to move on from opioid painkillers to heroin are likely to do so regardless of what laws are in effect. Said the study, "Some persons certainly use heroin when they are unable to obtain their preferred prescription opioid; however, whether the increases in heroin trends in the overall population are driven by changes in policies and practices regarding prescription opioids is much less clear."

Richard Taite, "Prescription Opioid Abuse: A Gateway to Heroin and Overdose," *Ending Addiction for Good* (blog), *Psychology Today*, November 7, 2014. www.psychologytoday.com.

Wilson M. Compton, Christopher M. Jones, and Grant T. Baldwin, "Relationship Between Nonmedical Prescription-Opioid Use and Heroin Use," *New England Journal of Medicine*, January 14, 2016. www.nejm.org.

in London, Ontario. "Lost in all of this narrative is the voice of the people who need it. If you live with constant suffering that's not controlled, you have relatively few options. You either turn to the black market and hope you can find stuff that can work—and how many people are really comfortable with doing that—or suicide, as the other option."[55]

Most Cases Are Not Black and White

Medical professionals such as Gullett and Walton insist that patients must be judged on a case-by-case basis and that blanket laws eliminating opioids from prescription assistance plans or regulations dictating how many pills can be included in prescriptions are not in their patients' best interests. Alison Block, a physician practicing in Martinez, California, says patients have come into her office in true fits of pain, and she has readily written opioid painkiller prescriptions for them. On the other hand, Block says, she has seen patients who are obviously doctor hopping or otherwise fail to prove to her they suffer from painful symptoms. She adds,

> But just as in much of medicine, the vast majority of patients do not align into black-and-white categories but instead fall squarely within the gray. Some have been on steady doses of chronic [opioids] for years, sometimes decades. They ask for refills month after month, and I grant or deny these wishes based on the unscientific combination of incomplete data and intuition.[56]

When it comes to deciding who should receive opioid painkillers—as well as how many pills should be prescribed—governments and physicians face many difficult issues. For every patient who lies to his or her doctor, there are certainly other patients, like Sandra Gartz, who take their opioids as prescribed. But as many doctors readily concede, even though their patients may be lying to them about their levels of pain, that doesn't mean they aren't in pain and deserving of drugs designed to ease their suffering.

CHAPTER FIVE

Prevention, Treatment, and Recovery

Andrea Steen was addicted to Vicodin. She pilfered the pills from her disabled husband, who tried in vain to hide the drugs from her. Sometimes, he was successful. Whenever Steen was unable to find her husband's bottle of Vicodin, she suffered through the ordeal of withdrawal—until she was able to find the pills again.

Finally, Steen came to terms with her addiction and decided to seek help. For most people addicted to narcotics, that usually means entering a drug rehabilitation program. But Steen is a resident of rural Marshalltown, Iowa. There is no local drug treatment facility in Marshalltown. To obtain the type of counseling that drug addicts need to help them kick their habits, Steen needed to travel to nearby cities such as Des Moines or Waterloo, each about forty miles (64 km) from Marshalltown. And since statistics show that many opioid abusers are like Steen—living in small towns or rural communities—Steen's inability to find a nearby drug treatment program is a problem faced by many opioid abusers.

But then Steen heard from a friend whose husband had also been addicted to opioids. Steen's friend told her that her husband had found relief from addiction through the use of the drug Suboxone. "She could tell when I was high," Steen says. "Her husband was on Suboxone. She was trying to help me."[57]

Suboxone is a drug developed in recent years that helps people addicted to opioids kick their habits. Suboxone and similar drugs work by attaching themselves to the opioid receptors in the brain, thereby forming a blockade that prevents opioids from sparking the release of dopamine. In July 2016 Steen received a prescription for Suboxone from a Marshalltown doctor. Steen's Suboxone prescription has reduced her dependence on opioids. Experts agree, however, that Suboxone cannot be the sole treatment for opioid addiction. In addition to taking the Suboxone pills, Steen also makes occasional trips to a drug rehabilitation center where she participates in group therapy sessions.

Going Through Detox

Tiffany Brackett of Toledo, Ohio, was addicted to opioid painkillers before moving on to heroin. A Suboxone prescription helped reduce her cravings for heroin, she says, but she also enrolled in a drug treatment program. "[Suboxone] is a tool to use with other things in your life, like going to [drug treatment] meetings," says Brackett. "It takes away the cravings and makes you feel normal without getting high every day and sticking a needle in your arm. But you have to go to counseling, meetings, get any support you can get. You can't just take the medication and get sober. There is a lot more to it."[58]

Drug rehabilitation is a very important part of helping opioid addicts kick their habits. For opioid users, the first step in drug rehabilitation is detoxification—in other words, flushing the drugs from the user's body. Time is, of course, the best method to rid the body of drugs so for opioid abusers, their challenge is how to remain clean and not return to opioid use during detox.

As opioid users go through detox, they may experience such symptoms as depression, lack of concentration, decreased appetite, fatigue, agitation, insomnia, sweating, nausea, trembling, headaches, muscle tension, and pain. For people addicted to opioids, the detox phase could last as long as ten days. It is such a difficult ordeal that many people addicted to opioids drop out of drug treatment during detox and return to abusing drugs.

In 2016 a woman living in the Detroit suburb of Farmington Hills, Michigan, told a reporter that she had been using heroin for ten years. The thirty-one-year-old woman, who identified herself as Amanda, started using heroin at the age of twenty. She transitioned to the drug soon after taking Vicodin pills that had been prescribed to her for a minor injury suffered in a snowmobile accident. When, finally, she resolved to give up heroin, she learned just how difficult her path would be. During detox, Amanda found herself suffering from deep moods of depression. "I'm not seeing what's so great about being clean,"[59] Amanda said. Soon, Amanda found she could not endure the depression and returned to using heroin.

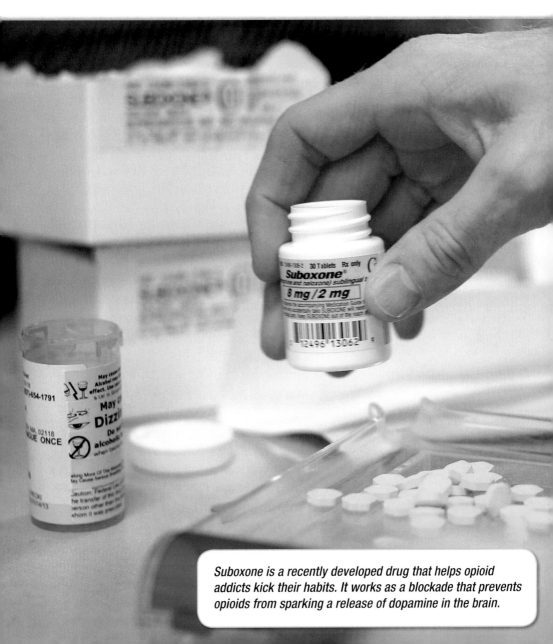

Suboxone is a recently developed drug that helps opioid addicts kick their habits. It works as a blockade that prevents opioids from sparking a release of dopamine in the brain.

Chemical Changes

For opioid addicts who do manage to emerge from detox, many challenges lie ahead. Merely going through drug detox does not mean the user will never return to opioids. Long-term use of opioids causes a chemical change in the brain, which is no longer able to release dopamine without the spark provided by opioids. Therefore, as most opioid users go through drug rehabilitation, they are unable to enjoy life. Occasions or moments that may have previously brought them enjoyment—such as a visit by a loved one—no longer provide fulfillment or joy because the brain is not responding with a corresponding release of dopamine. It could take a year or more before the brain is able to reverse the chemical change and act normally. Until then, many former opioid users find they have to endure fits of depression.

Says Joani Gammill, the nurse and former opioid abuser, "The more heavily a person uses, the longer the abuse, and the younger the person starts using all affect how intensely the brain suffers changes and how long it will take to heal." Gammill points out that young people may have a more difficult road to recovery than older abusers. Studies have shown that young people's brains continue to develop, usually into their early twenties. Therefore, she says, the opioids are making more dramatic changes to the brains of younger users because their brains aren't as fully developed. After younger users kick their opioid habits, she says, the damage may take longer to undo. She says, "When kids start using before the brain is fully formed in the early 20s, the potential is greater for lifelong addiction."[60]

Following the detox phase, drug counselors will often employ a treatment known as cognitive behavioral therapy, or CBT. Essentially, counselors work with users to learn the triggers that cause them to use opioids and then develop strategies to avoid those triggers. When working with a heroin user, for example, the counselor might learn that the user is most likely to take the drug when in the company of friends who are also users. Therefore, the client would be strongly advised to stay away from those friends because they may lead the user back to heroin.

Learning to Avoid Pain

For people recovering from opioid painkiller abuse, CBT may have to go a step further. After all, once users stop taking the opioids, they may still suffer from the same pain that caused them to abuse opioids in the first place. Therefore, counselors must find ways for former opioid abusers to endure their pain without the aid of narcotic drugs.

Certainly, avoiding activities that cause pain is one solution—a person with chronic pain caused by a back injury would be advised to avoid strenuous activities that might cause further pain, such as lifting heavy objects. But that might not be enough. People whose activities are limited by the pain they suffer often fall into states of depression. They find themselves unable to enjoy life fully, which makes them depressed—and candidates to return to abusing drugs. Counselors know they have to change people's attitudes, convincing them to look at life more positively so they

Talking About Pain

Many doctors are finding their patients are better able to manage the pain that afflicts them after surgery if they talk with them about how much pain they can expect, how long it will last, and what they can do to help reduce their pain. In the past, many doctors would simply write opioid prescriptions for their patients with the goal of eliminating all their postoperative pain.

Lewis Kaplan, a surgeon at a VA hospital in Philadelphia, says he finds it helpful to tell patients about his own pain, which he continues to suffer after surgeries he has endured. "I wake up with a pain score of six," he says. "This is an acceptable pain score for me." If he feels more pain during the day, Kaplan says he takes an over-the-counter pain medication, such as Tylenol. If the pain worsens as the day goes on, he might take some time to soak in a hot bath.

By talking about his own pain with patients, Kaplan says, he helps them find ways to manage their postoperative pain. Instead of prescribing opioids to most patients, Kaplan tells them, "Your expectation will not be zero pain."

Quoted in Stacey Burling, "Low Dosage," *Philadelphia Inquirer*, April 2, 2017, p. G4.

Drug counselors use a treatment known as cognitive behavioral therapy (CBT) to help their patients. This method teaches addicts how to recognize triggers that lead them to drug use, and how to learn to avoid those triggers.

may think about all the things they can now accomplish rather than the roadblocks that may stand in their way.

Counselors may also work with former users on techniques for relaxation and better sleep. Studies have proven that people who sleep more soundly suffer less pain during their waking hours. So simply getting a better night's sleep might reduce pain, and therefore, the cravings for pain relief from a drug.

Alternatives to Opioids

As former opioid users struggle to get their lives back, doctors, addiction experts, and government leaders agree that the simplest way to prevent opioid addiction is to make sure people are not given access to opioids. Because heroin has no known medical or other legitimate uses, the focus of these efforts is on finding alternatives to opioid painkillers. Many experts insist that alternatives exist and that opioids should be reserved for patients who are experiencing severe pain. Many doctors are also coming to believe that opioid prescriptions should not be their patients' first options. In 2017 the American College of Physicians (ACP), a professional association representing 150,000 doctors, issued a recommendation to its members regarding the treatment of chronic back pain: try other methods of pain reduction before prescribing opioids.

Instead, the ACP recommended that doctors tell their patients to try non-pharmaceutical therapies first. Among those therapies are yoga, acupuncture, meditation, and tai chi, a Chinese martial art that requires practitioners to move slowly while stretching their limbs. "I think most patients want medications as a fast fix," says Anita Gupta, a pain medicine specialist at Drexel University College of Medicine in Philadelphia. "What patients understand is often far from what the evidence tells us to do."[61]

> "I think most patients want medications as a fast fix."[61]
>
> —Anita Gupta, pain medicine specialist

When it comes to reducing pain for surgical patients, many doctors are now focusing on increasing dosages of anti-inflammatory drugs that help heal patients faster, meaning the patients should be spending less time in pain as they recover from their operations. At Canton-Potsdam Hospital in Potsdam, New York, seventy-two-year-old Pat Davis underwent two knee replacements over the course of six months. For the first operation, she was given doses of an opioid pain medication while still in the hospital. "I was kind of in and out of it, and I didn't want to get out of bed or move,"[62] she recalls. Six months later, she underwent the second knee replacement. This time, doctors focused on reducing the inflammation in the knee. She suffered no side effects, found she could manage the pain without the opioids, and recovered faster.

Medicinal Marijuana

One alternative to opioid painkillers that has gained traction among medical professionals in recent years is the use of medicinal marijuana. Over the past decade twenty-seven states have recognized that medicinal marijuana should be regarded as an acceptable alternative to opioid painkillers and have passed laws permitting its use. In Canada, medicinal marijuana has been legal throughout the country since 2015.

Statistics would seem to support the conclusion that medicinal marijuana is a viable alternative to opioid painkillers. According to a 2014 CDC report, the ten states where opioid painkiller use is lowest are California, Colorado, Wyoming, South Dakota, Minnesota, Illinois, New Jersey, New York, Vermont, and Massachusetts. In those states, physicians write between 52 and 71 opioid prescriptions per 100 people. In eight of those states, the use of medicinal marijuana is legal. (As of 2017, the use of medicinal marijuana remained illegal in South Dakota and Wyoming.) According to the same CDC report, the states where opioid use is highest are Michigan, Indiana, Ohio, West Virginia, Kentucky, Tennessee, North Carolina, South Carolina, Alabama, Mississippi, Louisiana, Arkansas, and Ohio. In those states, physicians write between 96 and 143 prescriptions per 100 people. Among those thirteen states, medicinal marijuana use is illegal in all but four states: Louisiana, Ohio, Arkansas, and Michigan.

> "It's a problem when we are replacing one synthetic opioid with another synthetic opioid because, guess what: synthetic opioids kill, cannabis does not."[63]
>
> —Uma Dhanabalan, physician and medicinal marijuana advocate

The fact that opioid use is generally lower in places where patients have access to medicinal marijuana has prompted many government leaders and public health officials to speculate about the use of marijuana, also known as cannabis, to replace opioids as the predominant painkiller available to patients. "What we are seeing is that, in follow-up visits, patients have decreased and even eliminated their opioids," says Uma Dhanabalan, a Natick, Massachusetts, physician who prefers providing patients with prescriptions for medicinal marijuana rather than putting them on opioid painkillers. "It's a problem

Opioid use is generally lower in places where patients have access to medicinal marijuana. This has prompted health officials to consider using marijuana as a possible replacement for opioids as the predominant painkiller.

when we are replacing one synthetic opioid with another synthetic opioid because, guess what: synthetic opioids kill, cannabis does not."[63]

A Gateway Drug?

As with opioids, the chemicals in marijuana attach themselves to receptors in the brain, which enhance the release of dopamine, making pain disappear. Lester Grinspoon, a retired professor of medicine at Harvard University in Massachusetts, said he discovered the pain-killing qualities of marijuana as early as the 1960s after his teenage son was diagnosed with leukemia, a cancer that afflicts bone marrow. Grinspoon said chemotherapy treatments—intravenous drugs that help kill cancer cells—made his son very ill and nauseous to the point where the treatments led his son to suffer devastating vomiting spells.

Finally, Grinspoon asked his son's friends whether they could provide him with some marijuana. The boy smoked the drug prior to the chemotherapy treatments, and was able to endure chemotherapy without pain and nausea. Although leukemia eventually claimed his son's life, the ordeal made Grinspoon into a believer that marijuana can be an effective painkiller. "We never—for as long as he lived—had to deal with that awful experience of seeing what he went through again,"[64] says Grinspoon.

Still, there are many skeptics who wonder whether medicinal marijuana could be an acceptable substitute for opioid painkillers. As with heroin, the 1970 US Controlled Substances Act classified marijuana as a Schedule I drug. As a recreational drug, it

How Naloxone Saves Lives

When Falls Township, Pennsylvania, police officer Nicholas Pinto was called to the scene of a drug overdose in a hotel room, he discovered a twenty-one-year-old unresponsive woman. He found her pulse weak and breathing shallow. Near her body, Pinto found a discarded hypodermic needle and empty plastic bag—clear evidence the woman had injected herself with heroin.

Pinto—as well as police officers in many other communities—routinely carries doses of the drug Naloxone, which he injected into the woman. The drug is similar to Suboxone in that it binds itself to the opioid receptors in the brain, thus preventing the release of large amounts of dopamine that occur with opioid overdose. Since Naloxone is injected, rather than ingested in pill form, it acts within two or three minutes to block the release of dopamine, which causes respiratory failure in overdose victims.

Pinto was able to save the woman's life, reviving her before an ambulance arrived to transport her to a local emergency room. Pinto says he has saved the lives of about a dozen overdose victims by injecting them with Naloxone. "It always feels good to save somebody," he says. "It doesn't matter what kind of circumstance it is."

Quoted in Jo Ciavaglua, "Police: Opioid Reversal Drug Saving Lives," *Doylestown (PA) Intelligencer*, February 4, 2017, p. A1.

remains illegal in all but seven states. Skeptics point out that over the decades, marijuana has long been regarded as a gateway or entry drug—in other words, the first drug many users try before they seek out other, more addictive substances, such as cocaine, methamphetamine, and heroin. "It might be an exit drug for some, or an entry drug for others," says Anil Kumar, a physician from Stoneham, Massachusetts. "If you don't have a way of monitoring this patient who is saying 'give me marijuana and I will stop taking narcotics,' they may do both."[65]

Nevertheless, given that more than half the states in the United States have legalized the use of medicinal marijuana, its potential for helping to end the opioid epidemic must not be minimized. For the past quarter-century, opioid painkillers have provided many patients with relief from intense and chronic pain. And yet, drugs such as Percocet, Vicodin, and OxyContin are widely abused, causing ruined lives, broken families, and overdose deaths. Meanwhile, heroin is no less a danger to people's health than it was nearly a century ago when the drug was first declared illegal. Government leaders and doctors have now recognized the dangers these drugs pose to the health of patients and must now weigh all available options to halting the opioid epidemic.

> "If you don't have a way of monitoring this patient who is saying 'give me marijuana and I will stop taking narcotics,' they may do both."[65]
>
> —Anil Kumar, physician who opposes medicinal marijuana

Source Notes

Introduction: The Victims of Opioids

1. Zachary Siegel, "Prince's Death Reveals What's Wrong with Addiction Treatment," *Daily Beast*, June 2, 2016. www.the dailybeast.com.
2. Quoted in Jessica Boddy, "Poll: More People Are Taking Opioids, Even as Their Concerns Rise," *National Public Radio*, March 3, 2017. www.npr.org.
3. Quoted in Teresa Carr, "Prince's Death and the Addiction Risk of Opioids," *Consumer Reports*, June 2, 2016. www .consumerreports.org.
4. Quoted in Carr, "Prince's Death and the Addiction Risk of Opioids."
5. Quoted in Joseph Pleasant, "Fentanyl: Deadly on the Streets but Lifesaver in the Operating Room," *WKRN*, March 16, 2017. www.wkrn.com.
6. Quoted in Pleasant, "Fentanyl."

Chapter One: A Problem of Epidemic Proportions

7. US Department of Health and Human Services, "The Opioid Epidemic: By the Numbers," June 2016. www.hhs.gov.
8. Edward M. Brecher, *The Consumers Union Report on Licit and Illicit Drugs*, 1972. www.druglibrary.org.
9. Russell Portenoy and Kathleen Foley, "Chronic Use of Opioid Analgesics in Non-Malignant Pain: Report of 38 Cases," *Pain*, May 1986. www.ncbi.nlm.nih.gov.
10. Quoted in Sonia Moghe, "Opioid History: From 'Wonder Drug' to Abuse Epidemic," *CNN*, October 14, 2016. www .cnn.com.
11. Quoted in Jessica Bliss, "Retired Nurse Couldn't Save Own Daughter from Opioids," *Tennessean* (Nashville, TN), December 17, 2016. www.tennessean.com.
12. Quoted in Bliss, "Retired Nurse Couldn't Save Own Daughter From Opioids."
13. Quoted in Pierre Thomas and Brandon Baur, "Waging War on Heroin in the Suburbs," *ABC News*, October 28, 2014. http:// abcnews.go.com.

Chapter Two: How Do People Get Addicted?

14. Joani Gammill, *Painkillers, Heroin, and the Road to Sanity: Real Solutions for Long-Term Recovery from Opiate Addiction*. Center City, MN: Hazelden, 2014, p. 11.

15. Quoted in Chancellor Agard, "What Is Percocet? An Addiction Expert Explains the Uses and Risks of the Popular Painkiller," *People*, April 27, 2016. http://people.com.

16. Gammill, *Painkillers, Heroin, and the Road to Sanity*, p. 18.

17. Bridget M. Kuehn, "Driven by Prescription Drug Abuse, Heroin Use Increases Among Suburban and Rural Whites," *Journal of the American Medical Association*, July 9, 2014, p. 118.

18. TheGoodDrugsGuide.com, "Heroin: Effects of the High," 2017. www.thegooddrugsguide.com.

19. Quoted in Foundation for a Drug-Free World, "The Truth About Heroin," 2017, www.drugfreeworld.org.

20. TheGoodDrugsGuide.com, "Heroin."

21. Cathryn Kemp, "I Was a Painkiller Addict," *Guardian*, September 9, 2012. www.theguardian.com.

22. Quoted in National Public Radio, "A Growing Number of Veterans Struggles to Quit Powerful Painkillers," *All Things Considered*, July 10, 2014. www.npr.org.

23. Quoted in National Public Radio, "A Growing Number of Veterans Struggles to Quit Powerful Painkillers."

24. Quoted in National Public Radio, "A Growing Number of Veterans Struggles to Quit Powerful Painkillers."

25. Quoted in Andrea K. McDaniels, "Hopkins Bloomberg Study: Parents Not Keeping Opioids Away from Children, Teenagers," *Baltimore Sun*, February 20, 2017. www.baltimoresun.com.

26. Quoted in *The Mirror*, "Talented Footballer, 16, Found Dead by His Mum Described as 'Having Everything Going for Him,'" January 16, 2017. www.mirror.co.uk.

Chapter Three: Living in the Grasp of Opioids

27. Sam Wood and Stephanie Farr, "A Heroin Hellscape," *Philadelphia Inquirer*, February 19, 2017, p. A1.

28. Quoted in Wood and Farr, "A Heroin Hellscape," p. A18.

29. Quoted in Walter Bird Jr., "Pill Man: One Man's Fight to Overcome Opiate Addiction," *Worcester Magazine*, July 17, 2014. https://worcestermag.com.

30. Quoted in Bird Jr., "Pill Man."
31. Quoted in Bird Jr., "Pill Man."
32. Quoted in George Dvorsky, "An Alarming Number of Kids Are Getting Their Hands on Opioids," Gizmodo, March 20, 2017. http://gizmodo.com.
33. Quoted in Caitlin Skvorc, "Former Addicts Work to Help Others Beat Substance Abuse," *Mat-Su Valley Frontiersman* (Wasilla, AK), March 13, 2016. www.frontiersman.com.
34. Quoted in Eric Adelson, "Star Athlete→ Injury→ Opioids→ Addiction→ Death," Yahoo Sports, March 28, 2017. https://sports.yahoo.com.
35. Quoted in Michelle Castillo, "Drinking Grapefruit Juice with Some Medications Can Be Deadly, Study Warns," CBS News, November 27, 2012. www.cbsnews.com.
36. Quoted in Kari Mozena, "Matthew Perry Talked About His Vicodin Addiction in Graphic Detail to Raise Money for Phoenix House," *Los Angeles Magazine*, June 15, 2016. www.lamag.com.
37. Quoted in Samantha Allen, "How Matthew Perry Forgot Three Years of 'Friends,'" Daily Beast, January 27, 2016. www.thedailybeast.com.
38. Quoted in Karin Johnson, "Airline Pilot, Wife Die of Suspected Heroin-Fentanyl Overdose; Kids Find Bodies," WLWT Cincinnati, March 20, 2017. www.wlwt.com.
39. Quoted in Kemp, "I Was a Painkiller Addict."
40. Kenneth Lin, "Lying to Receive Pain Medications Hurts Patients in True Pain," *KevinMD.com* (blog), August 28, 2014. www.kevinmd.com.

Chapter Four: Regulating Opioids

41. Quoted in Liz Monteiro and Anam Latif, "When Opioids Help with Pain," *Waterloo Region Record* (Ontario), February 18, 2017. www.therecord.com.
42. Joshua Landau, "How We Can Fight the Opioid Epidemic," *Charlotte Observer*, March 1, 2016. www.charlotteobserver.com.
43. US Centers for Disease Control and Prevention, "Guideline Information for Providers," March 15, 2017. www.cdc.gov.
44. Quoted in Ed Silverman, "CDC Issues Sweeping New Guidelines to Restrict Opioid Prescribing," STAT News, www.statnews.com.

45. Quoted in Maggie Lee, "Senate Bill Aims to Tackle Painkiller Overuse, Abuse," *Macon (GA) Telegraph*, January 30, 2017. www.macon.com.

46. Quoted in Amanda Hoover, "Chris Christie Wants to Limit Painkiller Prescriptions. Will That Cut Back on Opioid Addiction?," *Christian Science Monitor*, January 11, 2017. www.csmonitor.com.

47. Quoted in Hoover, "Chris Christie Wants to Limit Painkiller Prescriptions."

48. Quoted in Jan Hoffman, "Patients in Pain, and a Doctor Who Must Limit Drugs," *New York Times*, March 16, 2016. www.nytimes.com.

49. Patrice Harris, "Strengthening Partnerships to End the Nation's Opioid Crisis," American Medical Association, February 20, 2016. www.ama-assn.org.

50. Quoted in Nancy A. Melville, "Millions of Opioid Prescriptions Go to 'Doctor Shoppers,'" Medscape, July 23, 2013. www.medscape.com.

51. Jay Tracy, *Pain—It's Not All in Your Head: The Tests Don't Show Everything*. Victoria, British Columbia: Trafford, 2002, p. 84.

52. Norleena Gullett, "A Doctor's Take on Painkiller Abuse," ABC News, October 5, 2012. http://abcnews.go.com.

53. Gullett, "A Doctor's Take on Painkiller Abuse."

54. Quoted in Karen Howlett, "Ontario to Stop Paying for High-Dose Opioids," *Toronto Globe and Mail*, July 24, 2016. www.theglobeandmail.com.

55. Quoted in Paul Mayne, "Ontario's Attempt to Curb Opioid Addiction a 'Knee-Jerk Move,'" *Western News*, February 9, 2017. http://news.westernu.ca.

56. Alison Block, "A Doctor's Dilemma: Do I Prescribe Opioids?," *Washington Post*, June 10, 2016. www.washingtonpost.com.

Chapter Five: Prevention, Treatment, and Recovery

57. Quoted in Abby Goodnough, "Help May Be Thin on the Ground," *New York Times*, January 6, 2017. www.nytimes.com.

58. Quoted in Lauren Lindstrom, "Suboxone a Lifesaver for Addicts, with Caveat: Doctors Praise Drug 'Tainted' by Criminal Case," *Toledo Blade*, January 29, 2017. www.toledoblade.com.

59. Quoted in Eli Saslow, "How's Amanda? A Story of Truth, Lies, and an American Addiction," *Washington Post*, July 23, 2016. www.washingtonpost.com.
60. Gammill, *Painkillers, Heroin, and the Road to Sanity*, p. 19.
61. Quoted in Don Sapatkin, "Make Opioids Last Resort, Group Says," *Philadelphia Inquirer*, February 14, 2017, p. A2.
62. Quoted in Laura Landro, "Health Matters: A New Prescription for Surgical Pain," *Wall Street Journal*, October 17, 2013. www.wsj.com.
63. Quoted in Chris Villani, "Doctors Pioneer Pot as an Opioid Substitute," *Boston Herald*, October 4, 2015. www.boston herald.com.
64. Quoted in Cassie Shortsleeve, "The Truth About Medical Marijuana: Is It a Prescription Panacea—or Just an Excuse to Use?," *Men's Health*, 2013. www.menshealth.com.
65. Quoted in Villani, "Doctors Pioneer Pot as an Opioid Substitute."

American Medical Association (AMA)
AMA Plaza
330 N. Wabash Ave., Suite 39300
Chicago, IL 60611-5885
website: www.ama-assn.org

The AMA advises physicians on best practices for reducing opioid use among their patients. Visitors to the AMA website can find information on the AMA Task Force to Reduce Opioid Abuse, which discusses such issues as Naloxone, state databases that monitor opioid prescriptions, and guidelines for how physicians should prescribe opioid painkillers.

Canadian Centre on Substance Abuse (CCSA)
75 Albert St., Suite 500
Ottawa, ON
K1P 5E7 Canada
website: www.ccsa.ca

The CCSA monitors the abuse of alcohol and drugs among Canadian citizens. Many reports on opioid abuse and related topics are available for downloading on the organization's website, including its 2015 comprehensive report, *Prescription Opioids*.

European Monitoring Centre for Drugs and Drug Addiction (EMCDDA)
Praça Europa 1, Cais do Sodré
1249-289 Lisbon
Portugal
website: www.emcdda.europa.eu

The EMCDDA monitors drug addiction trends in thirty European countries. Visitors to the organization's website can download a copy of *European Drug Report 2017*, which provides an overview of the drugs that are abused in Europe, including opioids.

Foundation for a Drug-Free World

1626 Wilcox Ave., Suite 1297
Los Angeles, CA 90028
website: www.drugfreeworld.org

The foundation provides information to governments, individuals, organizations, and corporations on the dangers of drug abuse. Visitors to the foundation's website can read the series "The Truth About Prescription Drug Abuse," which provides descriptions and effects of opioid painkillers as well as heroin.

Kaiser Family Foundation

2400 Sand Hill Rd.
Menlo Park, CA 94025
website: http://kff.org

The nonprofit foundation conducts research on many public health issues, including opioid abuse. By entering the term *opioid* into the website's search engine, visitors can find many resources on opioids, including results of the Kaiser study "Public Opinion on the Use and Abuse of Opioids."

Phoenix House

50 Jay St.
Brooklyn, NY 11201
website: www.phoenixhouse.org

The nonprofit drug treatment organization maintains more than fifty programs to treat addiction in ten states. The organization's website provides many resources on opioids, including the stories "The New Face of Heroin," "Heroin Abuse Rises as Other Drug Abuse Falls," and "Fighting Addiction in Appalachia."

US Centers for Disease Control and Prevention (CDC)

1600 Clifton Rd.
Atlanta, GA 30329-4027
website: www.cdc.com

The CDC is the federal government's chief research agency that explores threats to public health. The CDC's website provides visitors with an overview of the opioid epidemic as well as steps taken by state governments and physicians to combat opioid abuse including the agency's 2017 recommendations to doctors on how they should prescribe opioids.

US Drug Enforcement Administration (DEA)

800 K St. NW, Suite 500
Washington, DC 20001
website: www.dea.gov

The DEA is responsible for enforcing federal narcotics laws. Visitors to the DEA website can find a text of the 1970 US Controlled Substances Act as well as many resources on heroin abuse, including several images of the illegal drug in its powdered form. The Statistics and Facts link on the DEA website provides statistics on drug arrests in the United States.

Books

Fareed Ayman, *Opioid Use Disorders and Their Treatment*. Hauppauge, NY: Nova Science Publishers, 2014.

Judy Foreman, *The Global Pain Crisis: What Everyone Needs to Know*. New York: Oxford University Press, 2017.

Joani Gammill, *Painkillers, Heroin, and the Road to Sanity: Real Solutions for Long-Term Recovery from Opiate Addiction*. Center City, MN: Hazelden, 2014.

Sam Quinones, *Dreamland: The True Tale of America's Opiate Epidemic*. New York: Bloomsbury Press, 2015.

Herbert Stephenson, *Junkbox Diaries: A Day in the Life of a Heroin Addict*. Chicago: Joshua Tree, 2017.

Internet Sources

Walter Bird Jr., "Pill Man: One Man's Fight to Overcome Opiate Addiction," *Worcester Magazine*, July 17, 2014. https://worces termag.com/2014/07/17/pill-man-one-mans-fight-overcome -opiate-addiction/25284.

Alison Block, "A Doctor's Dilemma: Do I Prescribe Opioids?," *Washington Post*, June 10, 2016. www.washingtonpost.com/opin ions/a-doctors-dilemma-do-i-prescribe-opioids/2016/06/10/be4 bb51e-2c31-11e6-b5db-e9bc84a2c8e4_story.html?utm_term =.0f67f7f80613.

Jessica Boddy, "Poll: More People Are Taking Opioids, Even as Their Concerns Rise," National Public Radio, March 3, 2017. www.npr.org/sections/health-shots/2017/03/03/518155165/poll -more-people-are-taking-opioids-even-as-their-concerns-rise.

Teresa Carr, "Prince's Death and the Addiction Risk of Opioids," *Consumer Reports*, June 2, 2016. www.consumerreports.org /drugs/prince-death-and-addiction-risk-of-opioids.

TheGoodDrugsGuide.com, "What Is Heroin?," 2017. www.the gooddrugsguide.com/heroin/index.htm.

Kenneth Lin, "Lying to Receive Pain Medications Hurts Patients in True Pain," *KevinMD.com* (blog), August 28, 2014. www.kev inmd.com/blog/2014/08/lying-receive-pain-medications-hurt -patients-true-pain.html.

Sonia Moghe, "Opioid History: From 'Wonder Drug' to Abuse Epidemic," CNN, October 14, 2016. www.cnn.com/2016/05/12 /health/opioid-addiction-history/index.html.

New York Times, "Inside a Killer Drug Epidemic: A Look at America's Opioid Crisis," January 6, 2017. www.nytimes.com /2017/01/06/us/opioid-crisis-epidemic.html?_r=2.

PBS, "Chasing Heroin," February 23, 2016. www.pbs.org/wgbh /frontline/film/chasing-heroin.

Eli Saslow, "How's Amanda? A Story of Truth, Lies, and an American Addiction," *Washington Post*, July 23, 2016. www.washing tonpost.com/sf/national/2016/07/23/numb.

Chris Villani, "Doctors Pioneer Pot as an Opioid Substitute," *Boston Herald*, October 4, 2015. www.bostonherald.com/news _opinion/local_coverage/2015/10/doctors_pioneer_pot_as_an _opioid_substitute.

INDEX

Picture Credits

Cover: iStockphoto/Back Yard Production

6: Associated Press

10: Maury Aaseng

13: Union army amputees recovering after surgery (b/w photo), American Photographer, (19th century)/Private Collection/ Peter Newark Military Pictures/Bridgman Images

16: Photo Researchers

22: Uwe Schmid/Okapia/Science Source

25: Thinkstock Images/iStock

29: Reuters/Newscom

32: Associated Press

37: Ryan Remiorz/Zuma Press/Newscom

39: Shutterstock.com

44: Associated Press

46: iStockphoto/Skynesher

50: Shutterstock/Lenestan

57: Brian Snyder/Reuters/Newscom

60: Thinkstock Images/iStock

63: Shutterstock.com/MWesselPhoto